Problematics of Sociology

Problematics of Sociology

The Georg Simmel Lectures, 1995

Neil J. Smelser

UNIVERSITY OF CALIFORNIA PRESS

Berkeley   Los Angeles   London

University of California Press
Berkeley and Los Angeles, California

University of California Press
London, England

Library of Congress Cataloging-in-Publication Data

Smelser, Neil J.
    Problematics of sociology : the Georg Simmel lectures, 1995 / Neil J.
Smelser.
        p.   cm.
    Includes bibliographical references and index.
    ISBN 0-520-20675-4 (alk. paper)
    1. Sociology—Philosophy. 2. Sociology—Methodology. I. Title.
HM24.S5318   1997
301—dc20   96-34335

Printed in the United States of America

1 2 3 4 5 6 7 8 9

CONTENTS

PREFACE

The event that precipitated the writing of this book was an invitation, extended in the fall of 1994, to be the second Georg Simmel Guest Professor at Humboldt University.

I accepted the invitation immediately, and was honored by it in several ways. First, it was an honor to come to Humboldt University, whose name is synonymous with traditions of academic excellence and innovation in higher education—traditions that still inhere in universities the world over. Second, it was an honor to be there at a special moment in the life of that university, which, after a long season of unwanted and undeserved intellectual degradation, has entered the period of revitalization that history owes it. Third, it was an honor to be in the shadow of Georg Simmel, one of the true fathers of sociology, though we do not always give him proper credit. Finally, I was personally honored—and humbled—in being chosen to deliver the Simmel lectures, and I would like to record my gratitude to those who had a role in bringing me there. In particular, I thank Professor Hans-Peter Müller of the sociology faculty, who extended the invitation, organized my stay in Berlin, was a model host, and commented insightfully on and improved the lectures.

My wife, Sharin, and I lived in the Humboldt University guest house for a month in May and June of 1995, the period set aside for the lectures.

It could not have been a finer location—immediately across the river Spree from the Bode and Pergamon museums. We were not far from the Reichstag either, where Christo and his armies were preparing to drape that building in its ambivalently regarded shroud. We also lived within a short walk of the Unter den Linden, as well as the Friedrichstrasse, now populated by hundreds of cranes and bulldozers, as the former East Berlin continues its remarkable transition. Humboldt University, too, is undergoing an accelerated transition as it moves forward aggressively to take a place of leadership in German higher education and simultaneously confront the dozens of ambiguities and ambivalences that its liberation and growth have occasioned. Colleagues were not too preoccupied, however, to extend us the warmest hospitality during our stay. Everything about that month made it an engaging and enjoyable interlude in life.

FOREWORD

It was a great pleasure and honor to welcome Professor Neil J. Smelser and his wife, Sharin, to Humboldt University in Berlin. We were glad to have him with us for a month as the second Georg Simmel Guest Professor. This professorship, in the name of one of the founding fathers of sociology in Germany, was established by the newly founded Department of Social Sciences at a reconstructed Humboldt University in 1993. In this year we celebrated the centenary of the first course taught in sociology at the Friedrich Wilhelms University, "Ubungen auf dem Gebiete der Sociologie," without a fee, by someone named "Dr. Simmel," as the course calendar informs us.*

Georg Simmel, one of sociology's major historical figures, studied and taught at Berlin University thirty-eight years without ever attaining a full professorship. There were a number of reasons for this: his professional success, his promotion of female students, his "modernity," his casual style, and anti-Semitism (Simmel was an assimilated Jew who converted to Protestantism). Somewhat belatedly, yet in his

---

*For full documentation, see the special issue of the *Berliner Journal für Soziologie* 3, no. 2 (1993), on Georg Simmel, edited by the Department of Social Sciences at Humboldt University.

spirit, we inaugurated a Georg Simmel guest professorship with a colloquium entitled "Berlin and Its Intellectual Culture" at which Lewis A. Coser, who has done so much for the reception of Simmel in the United States, received an honorary degree from Humboldt University on the occasion of his eightieth birthday and the sixtieth "anniversary" of his expulsion from Germany in 1933.

Actually, Neil Smelser needs no introduction. He is well known in Germany and famous in the Anglo-American world. Let me illustrate that by way of an anecdote. When I told a colleague in Berlin that Smelser was going to serve as the 1995 Georg Simmel Guest Professor, he replied, "Jesus, is he still alive? He surely must be in his late eighties!" Now, I can convince him that Neil Smelser is not that old in age and that he is still young in his thinking. But my colleague was not entirely misled; to the contrary, he gave ample evidence of how long Smelser has remained vividly alive in the collective memory of his German fellow sociologists. He referred to the famous book, *Economy and Society* (1956), which Smelser coauthored with Talcott Parsons. By that time, he had earned his B.A. in Social Relations at Harvard College, had studied philosophy, politics, and economics at Magdalen College at Oxford University, and was working on his Ph.D. (granted in 1958). So, before he finished his doctoral dissertation he was coauthor with Parsons of a prominent book that was translated into Italian and Japanese, but unfortunately never into German. In short: Neil Smelser was famous before he had a doctorate—unthinkable in German academic life.

Economy and Society and his doctoral dissertation, published as *Social Change in the Industrial Revolution* (1959), give us a hint as to the characteristics of his thought: first, a strong theoretical bent, which—given the impact of Talcott Parsons—does not come as a surprise; but from the beginning he struggled to resolve the problems and weaknesses of structural functionalism: Robert King Merton on the East Coast, Neil Smelser on the West Coast. He started teaching in Berkeley in 1958, where he remained until he moved to Palo Alto in 1994, to serve as the director of the Center for Advanced Study in the Behavioral Sciences at Stanford. Like Bob Merton, Neil Smelser retains the strengths while eliminating the weaknesses of structural functionalism. Instead of theorizing stability and order, he looks at social change and social movements; instead of accounting for order and change by abstract mechanisms like social control and socialization, he analyzes the precise dynamics of change; instead of dealing with individual actors and systems, he investigates collective action and institutional domains like the economy, education, and the family in a historical-empirical, not in an abstract-analytical, vein. The results are classics by now: *Social Change in the Industrial Revolution* (1959), for differentiation theory; *Theory of Collective Behavior* (1962), for research on social movements; *The Sociology of Economic Life* ([1962] 1975), for economic sociology; and quite recently, *Social Paralysis and Social Change* (1991). Theory is not a value in itself, but has to be taught. Among the numerous attempts to grasp the hard core of this impossible discipline I will mention only two: *Sociological Theory,* with Stephen Warner (1976), which I still regard as one of the best systematic histories of sociology, and *Sociology* (1994), which appeared as volume 1 of the UNESCO/Blackwell series in the social sciences.

A second trait of his work concerns the methodological side of the social sciences. In postmodern times favoring intuition, difference, and pluralism, this seems particularly outdated. Yet serious sociological analysis may very well profit from his reflections on historical-comparative methods. In this respect, I may only mention *Comparative Methods in the Social Sciences* (1976), which I consider still one of the most valuable sources for historical-comparative reasoning. At least this was a revelation for us as students in a remarkable seminar in Heidelberg with Reinhard Bendix, M. Reiner Lepsius, and Wolfgang Schluchter, when we studied Bendix, Barrington Moore, Victoria Bonnell, Theda Skocpol—and Neil Smelser.

Still another line of thinking emerges when we turn to the fields Neil Smelser investigated. First, economy and its hegemonic meaning in modern industrial society led him to plead for a true economic sociology, as *The Sociology of Economic Life* and *The Handbook of Economic Sociology* (1994), edited with Richard Swedberg, attest. Second, higher education and the role of the university in Western societies has repeatedly attracted his sociological attention. Let me mention the epilogue in Parsons's and Platt's *The American University* (1973) and the reflections in *The Changing Academic Market* (1980). Third, he has contributed to our understanding of the family. For a trained psychoanalyst who took psychoanalysis seriously while teaching sociology at Berkeley, this may not come as a surprise. This interface of sociological and psychoanalytical reasoning becomes visible in the book *Themes of Work and Love in Adulthood* (1980), coedited with Erik Erikson, in his portrait "The Victorian Family" (1982), and in the essay "The Historical Triangulation of Family, Economy, and Education" (1978) with Sydney Halpern.

But there is not only Neil Smelser the scholar, there is Neil Smelser the manager. It seems to be a trademark of this generation of institution builders like M. R. Lepsius and N. J. Smelser that they do not work entirely for their own fame but invest a great deal of energy in sustaining the discipline. Do not worry, I will not count the numerous committees and councils on which he has served. He played and still plays a crucial role in the social science establishment; he helped rebuild sociology at Harvard University, he was vice president of the International Sociological Association after our colleague Artur Meier, and is serving as president of the American Sociological Association in 1996–1997. He initiated the famous American-German Theory conferences in the eighties. One of the topics of these conferences was *The Micro-Macro Link* (1981). And it is the generic problematics of sociology—micro, meso, macro, and global sociology—to which the Georg Simmel Lectures in the summer of 1995 were devoted.

HANS-PETER MÜLLER
Professor of Sociology,
Humboldt University

CHAPTER ONE

Microsociology

In these essays I identify some central problematics of the discipline of sociology as I have come to view them over a lifetime of reflecting, reading, and writing in and on that intellectual field.

By "problematics" I mean those generic, recurrent, never-resolved and never-completely-resolvable issues that shape how we pursue our work, how we generate theoretical tensions and conflicts in that work, how we converse and debate with one another, and how we engage in that complex counterpoint of simultaneous advance, retreat, and repetition in our scholarship. The word "generic" also requires specification. I will not analyze the contents, internal tensions, and shortcomings of the work of any single sociologist or sociological point of view. Rather, I will focus on the philosophical, theoretical, methodological, and (occasionally) ideological issues that pervade sociological work, conversation, and controversy.

In carrying out this assignment, I will move through four successive sociological levels—the micro, involving the analysis of the person and personal interaction; the meso (or middle, or intermediate), connoting structural but subsocietal phenomena such as formal groups, organizations, social movements, and some aspects of institutions; the macro (or societal); and the global (or multisocietal). I assure the reader immediately, lest you suspect, that my choice of these four levels was not determined by the fact that I was asked to give four lectures. I chose them because they reflect commonly made distinctions in sociology, because each level presents some distinctive problematics, and because I myself have done sociological work that touches each level.

That being said, it should be recorded that I do not regard these four levels as embodying necessarily valid distinctions, or as reflecting some readily identifiable social reality. In fact, distinguishing among the four levels is analytically convenient at best and analytically mischievous at worst. On the convenient side, the distinctions yield a reasonable way of organizing a discussion of problematics; even here, however, there is a difficulty, because some problematics appear at more than one analytical level. On the mischievous side, the fourfold distinction lends itself to reification, to the view that the levels *are* separable and separate kinds of social reality. By this time we should know better than that. For example, the long-standing distinction between gemeinschaft and gesellschaft (a micro-macro distinction) has proved as troublesome as it has worthy in sociology, both because no totally satisfactory definition of either idea has materialized and because social forces emanating from both supposed levels constantly pervade the seamless social process. The troubles do not disappear, moreover, by reconceptualizing, as Jürgen Habermas has done, gemeinschaft as life-world and gesellschaft as the rationalized world of economy-bureaucracy-state. Moreover, I will note from time to time that a number of sociological problematics arise in attempting to define the relations and transitions among the different levels.

A GENERIC PROBLEMATIC: SOCIOLOGY'S INTELLECTUAL IDENTITY

I begin with a problematic that has, does, and will infuse all of sociology: its intellectual identity. Without hesitating, we normally refer to sociology as a social science. That is a misleadingly simple designation. Sociology, created out of and in the context of already-established humanistic traditions (especially history and philosophy), scientific traditions (both physical and life sciences), and aesthetic traditions, has never been able to make up its mind whether it is primarily scientific, humanistic, or artistic in orientation. Appreciating this, we can also understand the basis for many outside criticisms and internal divisions of the field. Let me elaborate.

- By the *scientific* orientation I refer to inquiry that focuses on natural laws and logically closed theoretical formulations; on causal, even deterministic analysis; on a dispassionate, objective, and nonevaluative attitude toward the subject matter under study; on empirical investigation; on precision and measurement; and on a method of inquiry that isolates and controls as many causes as possible to arrive at the decisive ones.

- By the *humanistic* orientation I have in mind inquiry that focuses on the human being; entails a preoccupation with the human condition (including human welfare, justice, equity, and suffering); does not hesitate to evaluate; and deals above all with human meanings, systems of which constitute culture.

- By the *artistic* orientation I refer to two separate connotations— first, an aesthetic posture toward subject matter, or an emphasis on pattern; and second, an emphasis on the application of knowledge, as in the "art of medicine" or the "art of the possible."

All three orientations constitute both the significant moral/intellectual *environments* of sociology and *parts* of the sociological enterprise itself. With this in mind, we can appreciate why sociology typically enjoys— better, suffers from—two types of experiences.

First, from outside, critics representing these orientations in their "purer" forms may react selectively to—that is, recognize some but not all parts of—sociology and assail the field for aspiring to what *they* represent, but failing to achieve it. Natural scientists frequently take on a bemused or hostile posture because sociology—or social science in general—pretends to be but is not truly scientific, that is, is "soft," which is shorthand for qualitative, imprecise, humanistic, and artistic. Humanists or those in the humanities may either find sociology territorially offensive, an intrusion on their traditional turf, or see it as arid and inhumane. Those who are artistically oriented find sociology ugly or useless, according to which of the two orientations of the artistic is invoked.

Second, from inside, sociology's complex composition—deriving from its neighboring and penetrating orientations from science, the humanities, and the arts—leads sociologists to raise doubts about their field's mission, unity, and identity and to foster recurrent controversies. Among these are the following familiar, overlapping examples.

- Sociology as value-free (scientific orientation) versus sociology as value-relevant (humanistic orientation).

- Sociology as fount of basic knowledge (scientific orientation) versus sociology as applied knowledge (artistic orientation).

- Sociology as agent of knowledge creation (scientific orientation) versus sociology as agent of ameliorative or revolutionary improvement of society (humanistic and artistic orientations).

- Experimental-aggregative-causal modes of analysis (scientific orientation) versus configurational-clinical modes of analysis (artistic orientation).

- Emphasis on positive facts and behavior (scientific orientation) versus emphasis on phenomenology or individual meaning (humanistic orientation).

- Quantitative analysis (scientific orientation) versus qualitative analysis (humanistic and artistic orientations).

In the American sociological tradition the scientific sides of these polarities have dominated. In fact, I can submit a working definition of that imprecise term, "mainstream sociology," as composed of those who, in one way or another, have tended to vote for the scientific side

of the polarities. As a rule, this mainstream side enjoys a dispropor-
tionate share of support and resources from university administrators
and external funding agencies, given the general dominance of the scientific ethos in American society. At the same time, there is no academic department and no sociological convention or congress in which
the larger scientific-humanistic and scientific-artistic tensions do not
surface in overt or covert ways. And, of course, different national and
regional traditions of sociology manifest different combinations and
balances among the several polarities.

MICROSOCIOLOGICAL ANALYSIS:
THE PROBLEM OF OTHER MINDS

The microsociological level includes sociology's version of social psychology, or the study of the person as oriented to the external, especially the social, world; processes of personal interaction; and the study
of small groups that typically but not always involve face-to-face interaction. It is important not to reify this definition. The micro level
shades into the higher levels: for example, the family is simultaneously
a primary group and an institution, and persons and interpersonal interaction make a difference at all levels of social organization. We ignore such admonitions for the moment, however, and move forward
on the assumption that the micro level constitutes a legitimate analytic
focus.

The micro level involves, above all, human beings (social science
investigators) directly studying other human beings (as they interact
with one another). This means that, under all but the most radical of
behaviorist approaches, we, the investigators, use our minds to study
other creatures with minds. (Even radical behaviorists do not escape
the assumption that investigators have minds, if they are to investigate!) A corollary is that there must be at least minimal communication between the investigator and others. This feature is evident in the
experimental study of humans, interviewing, participant observation,
and even in direct observation; it disappears only under conditions of

completely unobtrusive observation of behavior and the study of recorded precipitates of behavior. Even in those cases we are often said
to "converse" with our subject matter.

This observation implies that we cannot proceed with study without immediately exciting an enduring philosophical issue: the problem
of "other minds." The problem is a logical offshoot of skeptical philosophy, rooted in the works of Berkeley and Hume, who raised fundamental questions about our ability to assume the independent, enduring existence of all external reality, including the minds of others. The
problem was reactivated in the 1940s in a forceful statement by the
English philosopher John Austin ([1946] 1979). When the problem of
other minds is extended to the sociological investigation of persons—
both individually and in interaction with one another—it divides into
several subquestions:

- How can we know that others, including other minds, exist?
  This is the issue of skeptical philosophy proper.

- Even if we know or assume that other minds exist, how can an
  individual know about the nature and contents (thoughts, images, sensations, emotions) of minds other than his or her own?
  This is the problem of *verstehen* that pervades the Weberian and
  related traditions of sociology.

- On what basis (observation, imputation, empathy, projection) do
  we infer or attribute mental states to others? How can we have
  confidence in these inferences and attributions?

- What is the influence of our own minds (as investigators) on the
  minds of others, and vice versa, in the process of investigation?

- On what basis do interacting others know and take account of
  the minds of one another?

Many variations of and controversies in microsociology—and to some
degree in sociology as a whole—emanate from the different ways in
which these questions are answered.

For present purposes I will ignore the first question—the impossibility of the existence of other minds. For one thing, I do not have the patience to address, one more time, the question, How do we *really* know? when there is always room for enough doubt in contemplating the human condition to permit us to ask that question a hundred or a thousand more times without coming to a point of final philosophical certainty. Perhaps more important, it is fair to say that by becoming social scientists, we adopt an affirmative working answer to that question as a matter of occupational commitment; if we did not, we would be forever packing our philosophical luggage and never stepping on the train to take the sociological journey.

With respect to the role of the investigator's mind and the minds of others in the generation of sociological knowledge, the positions of Émile Durkheim and Max Weber—as expressed in their sociological manifestos—constitute a vivid point of reference. Durkheim's sociological positivism represents an extremely simple solution, in the sense that he attempted to define *both* as methodologically nonproblematical. He argued that if the sociologist approaches reality with preconceptions in mind, he or she distorts that reality. Instead, the investigator should cast aside such preconceptions and regard social phenomena as things, that is, as "distinct from the consciously formed impressions of them in the mind." The most important characteristic of a "thing," moreover, is "the impossibility of its modification by a simple effort of the will" (Durkheim [1895] 1958: 28). The investigator should free his or her mind of all preconceptions, take a passive relationship to social reality, and deal with phenomena "in terms of their inherent properties" (ibid.) and their "common external characteristics" (ibid., 35).

On the side of those being investigated, Durkheim took an equally positivist stance. He regarded individuals' "internal states"—such as motives, meanings, and emotions—as inaccessible to observation, and demanded that we put in their place some "external" or behavioral index that can be studied scientifically (Durkheim [1893] 1949: 64). He was hostile to the practice of appealing to psychological forces to explain social facts, going so far as to assert that "every time a social phenomenon is directly explained by a psychological phenomenon, we may be sure that the explanation is false" (ibid., 104). There is reason to doubt that Durkheim's own sociology was in fact presupposition-less, and there is clear evidence that he himself had ready recourse to psychological explanations, for example, in his analyses of suicide rates. However, his methodological position is clear: neither the mind of the investigator nor the mind of the investigated should—and, in the best of worlds, does—play an active role in the generation of sociological knowledge.

Weber contrasted with Durkheim on both counts. He insisted that scientific reality was not given in nature but was the product of a series of selections based on the investigator's interests and values. In investigating we select only those parts of reality that are "interesting and *significant* to us, because only [those parts are] . . . related to the *cultural values* with which we approach reality" (Weber 1969: 78). In thus asserting that any attempt to develop a sociology "without presuppositions" is "not only practically impossible—it is simply non-sense" (ibid.), Weber was saying, in our terms, that the investigator's mind must be regarded as active in the generation of scientific knowledge. Similarly, in understanding sociological reality, the investigator must also take into account the minds of the investigated persons. To appreciate this, one need only consult his definition of human action: "the acting individual attaches a *subjective meaning* to his behavior— be it overt, covert, omission or acquiescence" (Weber 1968, 1:4; emphasis added).

In making these methodological commitments, Weber generated two derived and fundamental problems.

- How can the investigator grasp the mind of the actor being investigated? To respond, Weber developed his idea of empathic understanding, or *verstehen*. Such a problem did not arise in Durkheim's methodological outlook, since neither the mind of the investigator nor the mind of the actor being investigated was thought to be problematical.

- How can the (presumably idiosyncratic) subjective meaning systems of different individuals be compared with one another, so that *general* statements, if not laws, can be generated in sociological investigation? To respond, Weber developed his notion of the *ideal type,* which entailed, in effect, assuming sufficient likeness or comparability of others' minds so that general constructions, such as "the Protestant ethic" and "rational bourgeois capitalism," could be characterized as sociological reality. Again, such a problem of comparing other minds with one another did not arise in Durkheim's positivism, because he regarded aggregation into general social facts as a matter of simply recognizing like items of behavior, or "things."

In a word, Durkheim solved the other minds issue by ignoring both these problems but in the meantime created a philosophically vulnerable methodology. Weber acknowledged the independent significance of the minds of the investigator and the investigated but in the meantime forced upon himself the need to develop formulations that would address the philosophical issues that he created by that acknowledgment.

Durkheim's and Weber's formulations represent two possible solutions of the other minds issue, namely, ignoring it and confronting it. While versions of the Durkheimian solution still remain in microsociology under the heading of social behaviorism (e.g., Homans 1974), most approaches and debates in microsociology confront the problem; as a result, differences in perspectives emerge in terms of *how* and *with what theoretical assumptions* to deal with the problem of other minds. The following types of "solutions" are evident in the literature.

- The utilitarian solution, found in classical economics, *endows* the actors being investigated with a material, self-interested motivational orientation and, in addition, *asserts* that this endowment coincides with reality, that is, that individuals are universally materialistic and egoistic.

- The "heuristic" utilitarian solution acknowledges that the rational pursuit of economic interest is not a psychological universal but assumes that that orientation is a powerful theoretical device in explaining market and other behavior.

- The "radical pragmatic" utilitarian solution, associated with the position of Milton Friedman (1953), allows that the postulate of rationality may be erroneous or nonsensical, but so long as it "works" in predicting economic results, it is justified.

- The phenomenological solution, considered generally, involves the claims that the meaning systems of investigated others do indeed constitute sociological reality, and that it is essential to discern these meanings to understand and explain that reality. There are a number of variants of the phenomenological approach. Weber's formulation of *verstehen* is one. I now call attention to several other related formulations.

(1) The ethnographic approach in anthropology and sociology is committed, in one way or another, to take into account the reports and accounts of informants and other actors in describing the culture and behavior of the society or group under investigation.

(2) The symbolic interactionist approach rejects the idea that the individual person is a passive vessel through which various social and psychological forces work, and insists that human behavior cannot be understood without taking into account how individual persons actively endow their internal and external environments with meaning and act on the basis of that meaning. The methodological implication of this position is that the sociological investigator must grasp, appreciate, and incorporate those aspects of meaning in any explanation of human behavior.

(3) The ethnomethodological approach also rejects the idea

of the causal significance of social structure and social roles, and insists that the behavior be understood as the product of continuous reciprocal monitoring of meanings and accounts of action on the part of interacting individuals.

(4) The dramaturgical approach exemplified by Erving Goffman (1959) entails a view of the individual actor as continuously manipulating meanings in social situations as a way of presenting himself or herself. While phenomenological in the sense that an understanding of this process is essential, Goffman also endows individuals with certain motives, such as status-striving, maintaining esteem, and maintaining consistency of self-image. In that respect his approach can be likened to that of rational choice theorists, who assume that certain preference schedules exist in the actors they investigate.

(5) Pierre Bourdieu's (1984) formulation of *habitus* as the individual's meaning-orientation system is an interesting phenomenological variant. On the one hand, Bourdieu criticizes economists' distortions of actors' orientations because they force upon actors *their* (i.e., the economists') preferred worldview. In this criticism Bourdieu suggests the desirability of a more appreciative approach. His own formulation of *habitus* is a multifaceted orientation that includes motivation, past experience, memory, and information.

(6) The methodological position voiced by some in the feminist and ethnic studies literature (sometimes called sexual and racial essentialism) holds that social investigation involves the sympathetic appreciation of others' situations and outlooks, and only those of their kind (women and minorities, respectively) are capable of this appreciation.

(7) An opposing methodological position argues that foreigners to a group have a special advantage in understanding its situations and outlooks, because they stand outside the taken-for-granted assumptions of those being investigated. ("The last creature in the world to discover water is a fish.")

- For purposes of completeness, one might mention "radical phenomenology," a position that maintains that reality inheres in others' meanings, but these are so inaccessible that they defy understanding by investigators. This approach is a completely skeptical solution to the problem of other minds, and, it must be acknowledged frankly, leads to a kind of methodological paralysis that appears to rule out sociological investigation entirely.

This map of approaches to the problem of other minds is sufficiently comprehensive to lay out the central methodological dilemmas involved. At one extreme, radical positivism solves the problem of other minds by denying its importance; the evident cost of this strategy is to distort reality by ruling out essential sources of determination in human behavior. At the other extreme, radical phenomenology solves the problem of other minds by submitting to it; the evident cost of this strategy is to render scientific generalization impossible. With respect to the intermediate strategies, the key issue is whether and to what degree the investigator actively *endows* meanings (including cognition, affect, and motive) to others and whether and to what degree the investigator attempts to *appreciate* or *grasp* others' meanings as they experience them.

In their turn, endowment and appreciation generate their own methodological dilemmas. Endowers provide themselves with the opportunity to generalize about others, but risk distorting others' meanings. Appreciators claim that they represent human reality more faithfully, but risk being caught in an ideographic trap, unable to break out of the idiosyncrasies of individuals' meaning systems and to generalize about them.

This dimension of endowment-appreciation is loosely—but not precisely—correlated with other aspects of social scientists' worldviews, though it must be realized that the following observations are impressionistic and speculative. Endowers tend to have a "hard" (scientific, objective, frequently quantitative) approach to their subject matter;

appreciators tend to have a "soft" (humanistic, subjective, frequently qualitative) approach to theirs. Endowers tend to "analyze"; appreciators tend to "identify with" and "respect." Endowers may be accused of "arrogance"; appreciators may be accused of "sentimentality." And, most speculatively, endowers tend toward a conservative mentality on a variety of dimensions, appreciators toward a liberal or radical mentality. Exceptions—such as the scientific Marxist approach, which is both endowing and radical—may test these assertions, but they do constitute food for thought.

At this point I would not be surprised if readers are not experiencing a certain impatience. It is all very well, you might be asking, for me to lay out this conceptual geography and note the difficulties of each of the solutions to the problem of other minds. That is the luxury of the critic: to identify problems in others' thought without oneself taking a stand on the resolution of those problems. Imagining your discontent, I will now lay out a series of assertions that I believe to be the correct philosophical and methodological guidelines for sociologists to follow in the study of individuals and their interaction with others.

First, we cannot adopt the radical skeptical position (either that other minds do not exist or that we cannot know them) or the radical phenomenological position (that other minds can be known only by those investigated). If we adopt either, we may as well turn in our identity cards as sociologists, because both positions involve, in effect, a renunciation of the possibility of knowledge about others. Moreover, in adopting either, the only role that remains for us is that of the negatively minded philosopher.

Second, we cannot fully externalize or deprivatize other minds by embracing a behaviorism that denies, ignores, or freezes the independent significance of humans' perceptions, affects, intentions, and evaluations. Under behaviorism I include both stimulus-response theories and rational choice formulations that rest on assumptions of fixed and stable preferences. The latter are, in effect, stimulus-response theories, because they explain behavior on the basis of knowledge of individuals' external circumstances (price, income, etc.). We need not embrace fully either symbolic interactionism or agency theory in acknowledging the necessity of taking into account the independent role of "internal" human processing of perceptions, sensations, affects, and intentions, as well as the adaptive alteration of behavior based on this processing.

Third, we should acknowledge that, as social investigators, we are agents, and that we must *endow* others with generalized motives, orientations, and capacities. This is a theoretical and methodological necessity in my estimation, for two reasons. (1) It seems a philosophical impossibility to reflect others' representations of their own minds without some independent act of interpretation; and that act, however minimal, entails the further act of endowing. (2) Unless we acknowledge the necessity for assigning *general* orientations to others, we are caught in a trap of methodological particularism and cannot hope to strive for general statements about our chosen subject matter. In other words, as social investigators we are forced, by theoretical and methodological necessity, to take the analytic step from the appreciation of the idiosyncratic to the typification of the general.

Fourth, in typifying others' orientations, we should not press the typifications beyond what they are—namely, constructed and admittedly distorted simplifications, necessary to proceed with investigation and analysis. Put another way, we should not reify or essentialize. Furthermore, the typifications must always be regarded as tentative and open to *empirical* investigation and conceptual manipulation. Suppose, for example, in studying social mobility, we assume, as an analytic starting point, that actors are guided primarily by orientations of status-striving—preferring a higher rather than a lower place in a status hierarchy. Some such typification is essential for analytic purposes. However, that typification should not be simply executed then forgotten. Independent empirical investigations (observation, interview, survey) can throw light on when such a typification is likely to be valid and useful and when it should be altered or abandoned. In a word, we should regard the act of analytic typification as a sociological problematic, to be investigated in the same way as any other sociological problem.

Finally, there are two reasons generic to the sociological enterprise why we should take a direct scientific interest in the typifications with which we endow others' minds.

(1) There is no formulation in sociology—micro, meso, macro, even global—that does not contain at least implicit assumptions and attributions about actors' assessments, knowledge, emotions, and motives. Durkheim, in *Suicide,* attempted heroically to live up to his methodological dictum that social facts are caused and explained by reference to other social facts. In illustrating this he linked types of *social* integration to different *rates* of suicide. Yet in case after case, we find Durkheim making theoretical sense of these links by referring to the putative psychological effects of, say, anomie, and to the putative behavioral effects of those psychological effects. Similarly, analyses of international finance strategies rest on assumptions about individual or corporate actors' motives or goals (to maximize profits, to secure conditions of monetary or political stability); and analyses of international politics consistently endow heads of state and foreign ministers with explicit game theoretical goals and strategy preferences or with some mix of motives of national self-interest, aggression, and peace seeking.

(2) One of the main vulnerabilities of every social science is that many explanatory efforts may degenerate into arbitrary or post factum formulations and accounts because investigators have at their disposal a *range* of possible psychological orientations (typifications) that can be attributed to actors. If "findings" do not seem to fit an explanation based on one assumed orientation, then the investigator might replace it with another, which presumably makes better sense of them. In other words, the range of assumptions about other minds constitutes a suitcase of possibilities, and the investigator is forever tempted to pick different items from the suitcase, as the occasion demands, to

make sense of anomalous or contradictory results of empirical research. All this is to underscore that the most careful and self-conscious attention be given to the kinds of psychological endowments that sociologists (and other social scientists) attribute to the minds of those they study.

HOW TO ENDOW: LIMITATIONS ON THE MODEL OF THE STABLE, ADULT, INFORMED, LITERAL ACTOR

Having established the necessity for the social investigator to endow the actor with psychological characteristics—all the while keeping that endowment open to revision in light of theoretical and empirical considerations—we turn to the next logical question: What should be the *content* or *substance* that we attribute to those we investigate? In other terms, what kinds of assumptions about human nature should we adopt to generate the most effective explanatory models of behavior and interaction?

We begin our response to this question with a familiar and identifiable image—the rational economic actor in the classical utilitarian tradition. There are two reasons for choosing this model: its simplicity and its radicalness. By the latter I mean that utilitarian theorists imposed very extreme conditions on the image in the process of making it simple.

The ingredients of the utilitarian model in classical economics are the following:

- By way of motivational assumptions, tastes are "given" for purposes of analysis; actors strive to maximize their pleasure—in this case their economic well-being—and act in accord with a few assumed psychological principles, such as that of diminishing marginal utility.

- The individual possesses complete information about the market.

- The individual operates in an environment with only a few

identifiable elements, namely, the price and quantity of goods available and the level of his or her own resources.

- The individual reacts to information literally, that is, does not make mistakes about it, does not elaborate it into complicated symbolic systems or otherwise distort it.

- Equipped with tastes, preference schedules, resources, and information about the market, the individual calculates correctly and behaves consistently.

- Others behave predictably and interact peacefully with the actor; actors do not coerce or defraud one another, and all occupy equally powerless positions with respect to their capacity to influence conditions of the market.

Such simplifying assumptions also enter into models that sociologists employ. The "role conformity" model of the actor found in some versions of role theory, for example, regards the individual as a socialized person, one who understands the norms and sanctions as they are presented to him or her, does not distort information, and is motivated, other things being equal, to follow the dictates of the normative system in which he or she is implicated.

We now understand enough about the process of endowing the actor with typified orientations to set aside the objection that those orientations do not constitute an accurate or adequate psychology. No typifications ever do. One can ask, however, about the conditions under which an assigned typification is useful as part of an explanatory model or theory. With reference to the assumption of the rational economic actor, my answer is a simple but unfamiliar and controversial one. It goes as follows: *such a model is most useful under those social conditions that institutionalize its characteristics and conditions.* A typical market for commodities is such an institution: it makes price levels and wage levels public, not secret; it institutionalizes choice and rewards calculation, in that it provides actors who calculate effectively with valued and disvalued sanctions (money, goods, commercial failure);

actors in the market are protected, more or less, by institutionalized laws against fraud and coercion. All this is to say that the validity of the typifications assigned by the economist to the actor is assured by the institutional conditions of the actor-in-situation, and, for that reason, predictions of behavior based on typifications under those conditions are likely to be powerful, because they reflect the realities of institutionalization.

In the history of their discipline, economists and others have realized that highly typified assumptions are not always valid, even in institutionalized market conditions. Correspondingly, much of the history of economics has been marked by relaxing the highly simplified typifications and then reconstructing models based on new typifications.

To choose a few examples of this: the theory of imperfect competition relaxes the assumption that individual actors cannot influence production and prices; economics as a whole has moved away from its earlier materialism and has introduced a whole new variety of utilities (prestige, power, self-esteem, etc.) that constitute preference schedules; many models of market behavior based on lack of information, uncertainty, and risk have been generated; and recent explanations are based on the assumption that when the costs of information and transaction become too high, economic actors invent systems of hierarchy (authority relations in organizations) and trust (in contracts) to minimize those costs.

What has given economics its *theoretical* continuity is its insistence on reincorporating the typification of rationality (including purposiveness, reasonableness, calculation, and self-interest), even after important parametric conditions have been relaxed. Enthusiasts of such typification, such as Gary Becker (1976), have argued for its universality, that is, its applicability to all kinds of institutional conditions (systems of justice and crime control, racial discrimination in labor markets, mate selection and family formation, fertility and other demographic behavior). That principle of rationality, even watered-down rationality, is the primary article of faith of economic analysis, and that principle survives even when the model of the rational actor is incorporated into the analysis of political behavior (Downs 1957) and the analysis of sociological problems such as conformity to authority and participation in collective behavior (Coleman 1990).

It is to economists' and others' credit that the limitations of the classical typification of the economic actor have been recognized and that relaxations and reformulations have proceeded apace. Those modifications have given greater flexibility and applicability to economics, though perhaps at the cost of theoretical determinacy. However, the continuing insistence on incorporating rationality as a typification has actually *discouraged* certain other lines of relaxation of the central postulates of economics. These lines concern mainly the nonrational and irrational sides of life, which, it can be argued, pervade all behavior including economic behavior in the purest of markets. The following examples of *omitted* relaxations come to mind.

- Active *distortion* of information on the part of actors. Revised economic models, as indicated, take account of lack of information, risk, and uncertainty, but not rationalization, projection, displacement, and other forms of distortion that deviate from the assumptions of actors' assessment of economic and social reality that are built into the economic models.

- The process of *symbolization* of commodities, work, and other economic phenomena, which endow them with systems of meaning above and beyond their reference to assumed utility preferences.

- The place of *affect* in interaction. In one sense this is an odd omission, because the original summum bonum of the utilitarian tradition was the seeking of pleasure and the avoidance of pain, which are, of course, matters of affect. In fact, however, the affects of anxiety, rage, love (especially blind love), neurotic

conflict, psychosis, and addiction (except when it can be explained as rational action; see Becker and Murphy 1988) do not
find a place in formal economic analysis.

To notice these systemic distortions in the tradition of economics and
elsewhere directs us toward ways of modifying the micro-level attributions we impose on our subject matter. To that topic I now turn.

THE INCORPORATION OF COGNITION,
MEANING, AND AFFECT INTO
SOCIOLOGICAL TYPIFICATIONS

I have just summarized and assessed the effects of the analytic bias toward rationality in the utilitarian tradition in the economic sciences.
Traditions other than economics have also contributed to diminishing
the affective, nonrational side of life. Marx inherited much of the utilitarian tradition and tended to subordinate all moral and affective sides
of life to the status of by-products of the objective forces of history,
though indirect references to affects—the misery of proletarianization
and the proletarian rage—are implied in his work. Durkheim, also a
thoroughgoing positivist, rejected "internal states," though his analysis of ritual and collective effervescence in religious celebrations takes
account of the vivid emotionality of such occasions. Weber's work concentrated above all on rationality and rationalization (though not in
the economists' sense of the term). He admitted the "affectual" as one
of his four fundamental types of action (Weber 1968), but aside from
its appearance in the analysis of charisma, the affective aspects of the
Protestant religion, and his remarks on disenchantment, the emotional side of life occupied a peripheral place. In general, then, as Alan
Sica (1988: 32) has concluded, Western theorists have not greeted the
notion of the irrational warmly "as a concept or as the root of an ideology . . . for some time."

A major exception to the rationalistic bias in social thought is found in the late nineteenth and early twentieth centuries in the work of Nietzsche, Freud, Le Bon, Pareto, Mosca, and Michels, all of whom stressed the nonrational and irrational sides of human life in different ways. But as far as long-term impact on the sociological tradition, Nietzsche has had little place, Freud must be considered marginal (particularly in comparison with his influence on the "culture-and-personality" approach in anthropology), Le Bon has been passé for decades, Mosca and Michels are remembered mainly for their contribution to the distribution of power in society, and Pareto is famous not for his residues and derivations (the emotional and ideological dimensions of society) but for his "optimum," a rational principle of economic welfare and social policy. Another major exception is found in the work of Georg Simmel, the only classical sociologist who even approached a sociology of emotion. While he insisted on a level of sociological reality (sociological forms) that is independent of psychological impulses, his own work gave open acknowledgment to the salience of the erotic and the emotional in many interpersonal relations (Simmel 1984).

The second half of the twentieth century has, if anything, accelerated the trend toward rationalist psychology and rational control in society. Consider the following developments as illustrations.

- In economics, the continued vitality of the tradition of rational choice. This perspective has also accomplished a major invasion of political science and has made minor incursions into sociology and anthropology as well.

- In psychology, the overwhelming success of the "cognitive revolution," with offshoots into cognitive science and information science.

- In psychoanalysis, the shift from drive psychology toward ego psychology and object relations theory, and the general decline of psychoanalysis and its insistence on the irrational role of the unconscious.

- The development of theories of rational management of the economy through monetary and fiscal policy, as well as the rationalization of approaches to business in "management science."
- The vast rationalization accomplished by the computer revolution in all its facets.
- Shifts in more specific fields of study, such as social movements, with the diminution of emphasis on affect and ideology toward the more rational emphasis on resource mobilization and strategies of social movement organizations (see chapter 2).

This family of tendencies in the social sciences—and more illustrations could be produced—has continued apace in the late twentieth century, despite the evident vitality of the nonrational in the postmodern world, which appears in new versions of alienation and disenchantment, mental disorders, conflict, violence, and a resurgence of primordialism in group attachments and political life.

I conclude this chapter by suggesting a corrective to the individualistic, rational approach—an alternative methodology for the study of social psychology and personal interaction.

SUPRAINDIVIDUAL CONSTRUCTIONS IN MICROSOCIOLOGY: THE EXAMPLE OF TRUST

At the beginning I defined the microsociological level as focusing on the individual person and personal interaction. Even within this circumscribed range, however, it is essential to distinguish three levels of analysis: (a) the psychological; (b) the intersubjective; and (c) the sociological, or systemic. In this closing section I explicate these distinctions, argue for their independent significance, and point out how all three are essential for explaining orientations and behavior at the microscopic level. Throughout I will use the idea of trust as a running example.

Trust has appeared in several lines of literature in the past two decades. In sociology, Niklas Luhmann (1979) and Bernard Barber

(1983) produced major, if preliminary, theoretical statements; economists have interpreted trust as a generalized way of reducing transaction costs (especially the costs of securing information and establishing the conditions of exchange) in market settings (Williamson 1993); in economic sociology trust has entered into the analysis of market networks (Granovetter 1985), the ethnic economy (Light and Kara-georgis 1994), and the informal economy (Portes 1994); and empirical analyses of trust have been ventured in areas such as the family, monetary attitudes, and litigation (see Lewis and Weigart 1985).

Trust is an evident and familiar *psychological* phenomenon, as revealed by the notion of a "trusting person." The attribute of trust connotes cognitive dispositions (expecting consistent behavior on the part of others), attitudes toward others ("people are basically good"), emotional dispositions (low levels of anxiety and hostility in interpersonal relations), and an openness of behavior that emanates from these dispositions. The typification "rational economic actor" implies a trusting person—one who accepts offered prices as honest prices and one who does not expect theft, violence, or fraud on the part of others. The idea of a "distrusting person" connotes outlooks, emotions, and behavior opposite to that of the trusting person. Goffman's (1959) typified actor appears to be something of a distrusting, even paranoid, person, always on the lookout for feint, sham, phoniness, conning, and "presented" rather than authentic impressions.

A number of lines of microsociological analysis focus on the problem of *intersubjectivity,* including strategies by which interacting individuals sustain predictable interpersonal relations ("trust," though it is not always named that) and repair those relations when they threaten to break down. The main image of interaction in the symbolic interactionist literature is of individuals engaged in giving off signals, interpreting and reinterpreting meanings associated with those signals, and mutually informing and correcting one another (Blumer 1969). The same model of monitoring taken-for-granted understandings and meanings is the focus of ethnomethodological analysis, with special emphasis on "repair work" that is done when conversation and other kinds of interaction break down (Garfinkel 1967; Schlegloff 1987). Goffman's dramaturgical games accomplish the same purposes, as do the processes of "frame alignment" (Goffman 1974; Snow et al. 1986), or the bringing of different persons' interpretive frameworks into agreement as a condition for interaction and the pursuit of collective goals. All these lines of analysis represent investigators' efforts to take account of the intersubjective processes that deal with the problem of other minds in interaction. Attitudes of mutual trust constitute "successful" outcomes of this kind of interaction, though other outcomes, including distrust, can be envisioned when the processes of trust generation break down.

At both the psychological and intersubjective process levels, the unit of analysis remains the individual, even when interaction is involved. Yet the analysis of trust and other aspects of interaction cannot end at this point. Processes of interaction—including two-person interaction—also have a *sociological* element, a systemic quality that cannot be generated by referring to persons and their psychological characteristics and cannot be reduced to or derived from these. In a word, trust becomes *institutionalized;* as such it has a sustained and reproduced reality of its own, independent of the psychological states of trust or distrust experienced by interacting persons. For this reason it is erroneous to treat trust only in terms of psychological expectations, "repeated games," or a condition sustained only so long as it serves the purposes of persons in interaction—for example, to reduce transaction costs—to be given up when it no longer serves those persons.

How should we characterize the sociological level of trust? The most evident instance is found in fiduciary roles, in which it is normatively expected, sometimes legally mandated, that people act in a relationship of trust to one another, even though they may not trust one another from a psychological or intersubjective point of view. But that is only the most evident example. Virtually *all* human interaction— even between blank strangers and between enemies—involves some level of institutionalized trust or distrust. Put differently, interactive relationships involve expectations about the following elements of trust.

- What is the *range* or *scope* of activities in which those interacting may expect predictable behavior on the part of others? In relations between strangers approaching one another on the street, the list is minimal and would include only expectations that the other keep a certain distance and not behave menacingly or as if out of control. Two drivers approaching one another on the road share expectations that are more complex, for example, that the other will obey the rules of the road as embodied in the highway code and will not make unpredictable or indecipherable moves with the vehicle. In neither example is there any expectation that the other will experience any specific affects: it is perhaps desirable to remain calm, but if the other driver is boiling with anger and that anger does not spill over into breaking the specific expectations, the affect is not relevant. The scope of activities to be trusted in more enduring relationships (among friends, lovers, or kin) is greater, and often calls for helping behavior, "understanding," psychological support, going out of one's way, *and* experiencing relevant affects.

- What affects are appropriate in the relationship? Some relationships (e.g., between cashier and customer) are neutral on this score; others (e.g., between physician and patient) call for the active suppression of emotion on the side of the one and are more permissive on the side of the other; still others (e.g., between spouses) call for the active expression of mutual respect, sympathy, and love.

- What is the *mix* of trust and distrust in a relationship? The institution of the market provides interesting mixes. Certainly, as Simmel ([1900] 1978) demonstrated, any market transaction is marked by a trust in the validity and value of the money exchanged (rules of "legal tender"). If this trust breaks down, substitute systems of trust (e.g., barter) may arise to take their place. At the same time, the idea of caveat emptor and the proliferation of practices such as giving receipts as proof of purchase, guaranteeing refunds, providing title deeds for property, requiring "truth in advertising," and affording legal recourse for cheating also indicate that distrust is institutionalized as well. Multiple marriages institutionalize "infidelity" without making it a matter of trust and distrust; monogamous marriages make sexual fidelity a matter of trust and often make infidelity a principal basis for marital dissolution; open marriages, at least in principle, institutionalize the denial of trust and distrust as marital issues.

• What are the rules of evidence that justify the inference that trust has been broken and legitimize expressions of suspicion and distrust, as well as the emotions of anxiety, shame, rage, and revenge? These affects, like all other aspects of institutionalized relations, are issues of normative regulation, and demonstrate the truth that no feature of social life, however private, is beyond social interest.

These aspects of institutionalized trust set the stage for interaction and constitute important determinants of how individuals define situations and react to them. Raising the question of institutionalization, moreover, calls out for the development of a complex classification of *types* of trust, based on the types of sociological relationships into which people enter—buyer-seller, politician-voter, parent-child, teacher-student, employer-employee, friend-friend. It also calls for the analysis of types of trust and associated expectations that informal roles—hero, fool, villain, scapegoat—generate. It also calls for modeling of benign and vicious circles of intersubjective trust and distrust, respectively, and of how these result in the cementing, alteration, or breakdown of institutionalized relations of trust.

Many interesting sociological situations arise under conditions of *discontinuity* among the three levels—psychological, intersubjective, and institutionalized—of trust. We capture such discontinuities in daily discourse by identifying the "gullible," who trusts more than the social situation merits; the "paranoid" (or what the French capture in the phrase *mefiez-vous*), who trusts less; and the "realist," who both trusts and distrusts and keeps an eye out for evidence of both. Democracy institutionalizes extended relations of trust and distrust between citizens and politicians. Under certain conditions (exposure of malfeasance, swings in public mood, shifts in standards of morality) the ground rules for what constitutes trustworthiness and untrustworthiness may shift and redefine the political process. Under such circumstances, moreover, intersubjective trust between citizen and politician forever threatens to break down into mutual distrust.

The objective of this exploration of the different levels of psychological and sociological trust is to demonstrate that (a) the sociological mode of analysis is not different at the microsociological level than it is at higher levels of social organization; indeed it penetrates the most intimate levels of interaction; (b) regularities of behavior cannot be understood or explained without reference to the sociological dimension; and (c) the psychological, intersubjective, and institutional levels must incorporate affective and other "nonrational" ingredients. We might even say that the model of sociologically naive actors—as in rational choice and game theoretical models—are misguided for almost all occasions. Our typifications and explanations must involve the continuous interaction of institutionalized expectations, perceptions, interpretations, affects, distortions, and behavior.

CHAPTER TWO

Mesosociology

About five years ago a group of American sociologists formed a group they called MESO, endowing it with its literal meaning, middle. The group is an informal one; it does not publish a journal. By now it has about two hundred members, and meets once a year for presentation and discussion of papers. It grew out of a dissatisfaction among a number of students of formal organization with the micro-macro distinction, a distinction that gained currency in the 1980s (see Collins 1981; Alexander et al. 1987). They felt that that distinction distorted their world of study—the middle—and that the middle constitutes a crucial link between the psychological and the societal. The focus of the group is—though not in a very deliberate or coherent way—on the meso-level phenomena identified at the beginning of the first chapter: groups, formal organizations, social movements, and some aspects of institutions.

Of the four levels that constitute my subject matter, the meso-level is the most vague. It seems most helpful to delineate it by instances rather than by formal definition. It concerns what Tocqueville ([1835] 1945) referred to as "associations"; it includes that level of society identified by mass society theorists (Kornhauser 1959) as "intermediary"—community life, voluntary associations, trade unions, and political parties; it overlaps with what political scientists and others refer to as civil society, that complex of political groups and institutions that mediate between the citizenry (micro) and the polity (macro) (Putnam 1993). Because of this vagueness of reference of "meso," a few clarifying theoretical remarks are in order at the outset.

ANALYTIC LEVELS AND THE PROBLEM OF REDUCTION

Early in the last chapter I mentioned the danger of reifying the organizational principles on which these essays are based. Even though the micro, meso, macro, and global levels can be identified, it must be remembered that in any kind of social organization we can observe an interpenetration of these analytic levels. This can be illustrated by reference to a "meso-level" structure, a bureaucratic organization. Evidently such an organization lies "between" interacting individuals and larger societal structures. Any bureaucratic organization is populated by individuals (micro level) and is regulated by laws and other normative systems—for example, laws of charter and incorporation, standards of accountability—and legitimated by at least implicit reference to cultural standards and values (macro level).

Despite the soundness of this observation, we social scientists appear to be programmed with a certain bias when relating different analytic levels to one another: the bias of methodological individualism. We live in the Western cultural tradition, which has exploited the cultural values of individualism. As children of that tradition, we are most comfortable taking the individual person as the starting point of analysis. Put another way, that cultural tradition "tilts" us toward assuming that the natural unit for the behavioral and social sciences is the individual. The same tilt informally discourages the recognition of *other* levels of social organization as equally natural. There is reason to believe, however, that other levels of reality are analytically as important as—more important for some purposes—the person. I now venture a few observations on this score.

For those lines of inquiry rooted most firmly in the individualist tradition—I have in mind psychology (the study of the person) and the Anglo-American discipline of economics—the individual is the basic unit of analysis, and the movement to higher levels of organization is frequently a matter of aggregation of individuals. That has been the main mode of transition between microeconomics and macroeconomics, with markets and whole economies (e.g., gross domestic product) being treated as summations of thousands or millions of individual transactions. In survey research we add and percentage *individual* responses to survey questions and imagine that we have measured "public opinion." In a social psychological expression of this principle of methodological individualism, Floyd Allport (1924) argued that the crowd mentality and crowd behavior are nothing more than the aggregation of individual characteristics. Interestingly, Simmel flirted with the same notion in one of his definitions of society. Society, he said, in "only the name of the sum of [social] interactions. . . . It is therefore not a unified, fixed concept by rather a gradual one, . . . a constellation of individuals" (quoted in Frisby 1990: 17). This observation did not exhaust Simmel's treatment of society, but it is a vivid statement of the logic that the whole is the sum of its parts.

Another intellectual strand in the sociological tradition has attempted to establish the analytic value of more comprehensive levels of reality. One crude attempt was that of Gustav Le Bon, who asserted that the crowd exhibits a qualitatively new mentality from that of its individual members. The notion of a higher sociological reality is also at the heart of Durkheim's *Rules* ([1895] 1958), which constituted simultaneously a claim that there exists, sui generis, a supraindividual society with distinctive characteristics and a claim on behalf of sociology as the science of that society. Simmel also developed a version of this appeal. In his identification of prototypical sociological forms— for example, dominance or competition—he argued that such forms were analytically independent of both the psychological characteristics of individuals involved and their cultural context. Finally, in a formulation influenced by Simmel's idea of form (Kaern 1990), Weber attempted to build a supraindividual level of reality in his conception of "ideal types," though he regarded these as abstractions from the individual meaning-experiences of actors. All of these supraindividual formulations have enjoyed only fragile, impermanent status, and all have been subject to various forms of criticism, stemming, I submit, from the fundamental preference for methodological individualism in our traditions of social thought. Accordingly, the temptation to fall into psychological—or rather, individual—reductionism is alive and well in the social sciences.

My own effort to resolve this problematic has always been to insist on the conceptual validity of higher levels of formulation—interaction, group, organization, institution, society, even multisociety—not on grounds of any absolute philosophical claims to reality but on essentially programmatic grounds: it is impossible to understand and explain events, situations, and processes of "lower" units without appealing to some higher order of organization by which they are constrained. Physics requires its chemistry, chemistry its biochemistry, biochemistry its biological organism, biological organism its integrative mental processes, and individuals their social organization, if we are to proceed beyond atomistic characterizations and understand more complex behaviors and sequences. This acknowledgment does not call for any special assertions about reality, but rests on the need for higher-level organizing constructs necessary for comprehensive explanations.

MECHANISMS LINKING THE INDIVIDUAL AND MESO-LEVEL STRUCTURES

One argument for focusing on the meso level is that structures at that level constitute the primary bases for organizing the routines, interactions, and affective linkages of individuals' daily lives. As individuals we connect daily with the larger society via the groups, organizations (places of employment, unions, churches), associations, and social movements of which we are members. This range of life is what Simmel (1965) had in mind in his concepts "circles" and "web of group affiliations." Through these linkages social life becomes real to the individual, certainly more real than his or her relationship with institutions, systems of institutions, and social classes, to say nothing of the state, the society, and the international order. This point makes general the assertion, familiar to political scientists, that the success of political democracy depends as much on the specifics of civil society (that network of intermediate, or meso, organizations lodged between individual and polity) as it does on the formal institutions of the polity. It is in the more intimate structures that the civic culture is learned and given vitality.

This observation leads immediately to the question of the mechanisms that bind individuals to the groups, organizations, and associations. Why do they attach to them? This is simultaneously a question of motivation and a question of incentives, or, in a phrase familiar to the sociologist, a question of *socially structured motivation:* learned and normatively articulated orientations of individuals toward their group and organizational environment.

In keeping with our inherited individualist-utilitarian frame, it seems—but only seems—easier to think about this problem in some contexts more than others. If we ask, for example, what ties individuals (workers) to organizations that employ them, we typically turn to the following kind of explanation: the employer offers wage payments to individuals, who, in return, provide labor and cede to the employer a measure of control over their time and independence. Whether this constitutes a mutually beneficial contractual agreement (as in classical political economy) or an instance of exploitation (as in Marxian economics) seems secondary. The actual mechanism is identical, whatever the interpretation assigned. Furthermore, we are comfortable with the idea that reference to these mechanisms constitutes a sufficient account of the motivation-and-incentive situation at hand. I would suggest, however, that the *reason* we are comfortable with such an account is that this interplay of motivation and incentives is deeply institutionalized in the money-market complex of contemporary society.

Furthermore, so embedded is this complex of institutions and assumptions that it sometimes creates intellectual puzzles that are analytically unnecessary. Consider, for example, the issue of why people join social movements. We will observe later that in the study of such movements many "reasons for joining"—imitation, contagion, suggestibility, ideological commitment, expressive gratification, the need for solidarity, among others—have been generated. If, however, we approach the problem within the individualistic-utilitarian perspective, we are likely to generate unwanted paradoxes and unnecessary resolutions of those paradoxes because—*within that framework*—individuals are seen as having no reason to join social movements since a cost-benefit analysis yields no plausible motive to participate. It is only in this context—not as a completely general matter—that the "free rider" and related paradoxes arise, and *induce* scholars operating within the individualistic-utilitarian tradition (e.g., Olson [1965], Oberschall [1973], and Coleman [1990]) to generate complex cost-benefit schemes to account for why individuals affiliate with and participate in social movements and social movement organizations.

It might prove worthwhile to break from the individualistic-instrumental-rational set of assumptions that generate that statement of the problem and its attempted solutions. We might then turn to a different definition of the situation, to identify *other* socially structured types of motivation and treat these as equally valid bases for generating models linking individuals to meso-level structures.

One starting point would be to revive earlier efforts by Talcott Parsons and his associates (e.g., Parsons and Smelser 1956; Parsons 1963a, 1963b, 1968) to identify "generalized media," of which the main types are money, power, influence, and value-commitments. Parsons treated these media mainly as mechanisms that facilitated exchange and equilibrium at the social system level. They can, however, also be regarded as socially structured motivational complexes that form the basis for individuals' affiliation with groups, organizations, and movements. They constitute simultaneously types of motivations and types of incentives or rewards. For understandable reasons, Parsons's formulation of wealth and power attained greater analytic clarity than did the treatment of influence and value-commitments. It is clear, however, that influence is a motivation that combines sociability, expressive gratification, and appeal to common membership; and that value-commitment is a motivation that links the continuity of individual identity, attitudes, and values to cultural patterns. These constitute motivational-incentive complexes for linking with social organizations as much as wealth and power do. Furthermore, there is no reason for sacrificing analytic power in appealing to them. By positing models based on these complexes, it remains possible to generate rigorous explanations of individual participation in the more expressive and affective sides of social life.

MESO-LEVEL STRUCTURES

In the remainder of the chapter I will touch on the four sets of structures identified as "meso"—groups, formal organizations, social movements, and institutions—and point to a number of problematics for each.

Groups

Groups, especially expressive groups, have become something of a casualty in the recent history of sociology, despite their notable place in both sociology and social psychology. Simmel's pioneering work on group size and group process (Wolff 1950: 87–177) is itself a notable part of that tradition.

The golden age of the group was the 1940s and 1950s, when the informal group was recognized as a salient force in industry (Roethlisberger and Dickson 1939), in the military (Shils and Janowitz 1948), in community action (Lewin 1948), in market and voting behavior (Katz and Lazarsfeld 1955), in disaster behavior (Killian 1952), and in sociological theory generally (Homans 1951). This concern has, by and large, fallen by the wayside. The efflorescence of innovative experimental studies on group interaction and process (e.g., Bales 1950; Leavitt 1951) has likewise subsided. Similarly, the family as site of group process has given way to the themes of family as institutional victim (in the family literature) and family as vehicle for dominance and subordination (in the feminist literature).

This is not the moment to develop a sociology of knowledge about this decline, but the following factors may be mentioned.

- The surge of macrosociological interest (mainly neo-Marxian, neocritical, and neo-Weberian) in the 1960s and 1970s, with its attendant focus on macro-level domination.

- The failure of the "microsociological revolution" (symbolic interactionism, ethnomethodology, phenomenology generally) in the 1970s and agency theory subsequently to move beyond the person and personal interaction and to revitalize an interest in group processes as such.

- The "system" focus that dominates feminist sociology and race relations research.

- The institutional—not the group—focus of the "new institutionalisms" in economics, sociology, political science, and history.

The group does survive as a tradition in experimental social psychology, and Habermas's theoretical interest in the life-world processes reminds us of the importance of the face-to-face group, but his interest has been in group interaction as a counterforce to the colonizing tendencies of the market-state-bureaucratic apparatus, not in group life as such.

One additional factor might be evoked in explaining the decline of interest in groups, and this factor points toward a new line of inquiry. I suggest that, because of accelerating economic and social developments in the world, the group as it was conceptualized in the "golden age"—a relatively stable, enduring, face-to-face, cooperative unit—has, *as a matter of institutional fact,* receded dramatically by the end of the twentieth century. The developments that have occasioned this recession, moreover, are those that Simmel originally identified in his imaginative depiction of the metropolis—the enhanced "individuation of the individual" through social and economic mobility, fleeting contacts dictated by the pace of life, segregation of social circles through further differentiation, and the resulting experiences of isolation, freedom, and a blasé mentality. All these have eclipsed the primary group as we knew it. And that is one of the major reasons we pay less attention to it.

That is not the final answer, however. The group remains important in contemporary society, but operates according to a different principle. The image I have in mind is the "fission-fusion" principle that has been identified as a principle of bonding in the group life of seagoing mammals and primates (Wrangham and Smuts 1980; Symington 1990; Smolker et al. 1992). That principle involves the frequent coming together of social groups in apparently meaningful form for the animals, but it is accompanied by an equally apparent tendency for these groups to dissolve—or dissolve partially—only to re-form in new but also impermanent combinations. This fission-fusion principle has accelerated dramatically in *human* life as well at the end of the twentieth century. The instability of group life—in the workplace, on the street corner, in the office, and in the family—is now more the rule, and stability is more the exception.

To acknowledge this is not to say that groups have receded in importance in the human condition. They remain central and crucial. They still express the fundamental—perhaps genetically fixed—tendencies to bond with others and to be socially dependent in the human condition. These tendencies need now to be studied more intensively, however, in their relatively fleeting—rather than permanent—form.

New understandings and new models of this accelerated fission-fusion principle are required. In rising to this new kind of understanding, we also need to understand whether—and if so, in what ways—the human predisposition for bonding is being taxed to the point of generating serious social costs. In the following chapters I will underscore the increased salience and assertiveness of subnational groupings based on race, ethnicity, region, language, and other "local" forces. It may well turn out that these tendencies are expressions, in part, of a reassertive reaction to the erosion of human bonding occasioned by the acceleration of the fission-fusion principle in contemporary social life.

Formal Organizations

Max Weber established the principle that formal organizations are the structural signature of the rise of industrial capitalism. Weber also affirmed that bureaucracies were not a child exclusively of capitalism, but predicted, correctly, that socialism would only further the march of bureaucracy, largely, we suspect, because of the premium that socialism gives to government ownership and management. We might even extend Weber. Whatever the transition from industrial to post-industrial might mean, it certainly has brought the further consolidation of formal organizations in the lives of individuals and societies. If anything, the past decades have seen the transition from discrete organizations to multiorganizational *systems*—expanded civil service bureaucracies, multinationally coordinated corporations, multicampus universities, and ecumenical formations of churches.

In the scholarly work on organizations we discern three recurrent and overlapping problematics: organizations as efficient or inefficient, organizations as adaptive or maladaptive, and organizations as closed or open systems.

- Two major traditions of organizational study—the theory of the firm in economics and Weber's theory of bureaucracy—established the notion that bureaucracies are efficient, though the logic leading to that conclusion was different in each tradition. In classical economics, the firm was a kind of black box, essentially without internal organization, that responded rationally to the markets for the factors of production on the one side and the markets for the firm's products on the other, producing equilibrium market solutions in the process. Weber turned to the internal organization of bureaucracies—hierarchy, authority through rules, division of labor, and written procedures—to locate their comparative advantage over staff organizations based on charisma and tradition. Two subsequent lines of inquiry have challenged the efficiency assumption—the insight that informal groups can systematically undermine the formal purposes of organizations and the long-standing popular and scholarly appreciation of the debilitating power of bureaucratic encumbrances such as red tape and procedures for procedures' sake (Parkinson 1957).

- Most traditions in organizational sociology treat the organization as adaptive, or as at least striving to be adaptive. However, the field has proceeded beyond earlier assumptions, built into both the classical economic and the Weberian traditions, to an extensive literature that takes adaptation as problematical, and considers conditions such as information, technology, competitive environment, organizational culture, age and size of organization, and internal structure as determinants of adaptation or maladaptation (Aldrich and Marsden 1988). One notable model is the "garbage can model of organization choice" (Cohen, March, and Olsen 1972) that treats decision making as calling up strategies selectively from a loosely organized reservoir of criteria and possibilities. (The model foreshadows Swidler's [1986] "reservoir" theory of culture.) I call attention to this model because, although it lies in the "adaptive" tradition, it breaks from the dominant assumptions of rationality that have dominated organization theory. The "garbage can" or "reservoir" models may be appropriately criticized on one set of grounds: although eminently realistic as an account of decision makers' activities in organizations—for what are decision makers if not people who try to make use of all resources, strategies, and tactics that they believe to be at their disposal?—the model is also highly indeterminate because it incorporates only "flexibility" as preference function. It seems an appropriate strategy for theorists of organization to build such flexibility into their psychological assumptions about decision making, but they should also take the opportunity to generate submodels for the organizational and environmental conditions under which different strategies might be selected.

- The earlier "closed systems" approach to organizations, also associated with the classical schools, gave way in midcentury to a stress on "natural systems." By now most research assumes that formal organizations are implicated in complex environments composed of differentially available technology, different qualities of information, other organizations, and legal and regulative systems.

I mention the dimension of "openness" because two of the most important recent trends in the organizational literature focus on the institutional, competitive, and technological environments of organizations. The first goes by the name of "the new institutionalism" in sociology (Powell and DiMaggio 1991), which has revived and modified the notion of the penetration and reproduction of institutional forces in organizations. Its major focus is on the cultural routines and scripts that are invoked as orienting symbols, constraints on choice and rationality, and stabilizing forces. The second approach involves the idea that new competitive and technological forces—especially in the global setting—are pushing toward radically different forms of organization to such a degree that formal organizations—like primary groups—are undergoing such fundamental changes that they demand completely new foci of analysis. Transaction cost analysts have raised the question whether hierarchy (authority) in organizations—the hallmark of classical Weberian theory—is not in many instances too costly a structure (Williamson 1985). There is also a small, enthusiastic literature on new organizational forms that has produced a flurry of catchwords—"flexible specialization" (Piore and Sabel 1984), networks, self-managed teams, "adhocracy," franchise organizations, consortia, partnerships, and even "virtual organizations"—all of which suggest that loose, cooperative, informal, continuously re-created organizations are coming to replace authority-based organizations with a specialized, detailed, and fixed division of labor (Fordism). One influential model to have emerged from this line of thinking is the "contingency model," which also is meant to describe the weakening of hierarchy, authority, and specified rules and procedures: "Rapidly changing environments and uncertain technology, such as characterized the electronics industry, . . . appeared to produce organizations with adaptive, free-flowing, 'organic' structures. The organic structure emphasized employee interactions, horizontal as well as vertical communication, and greater professional autonomy in which employees 'discovered' rather than were assigned to their jobs" (Dill and Sporn 1996, after Lawrence and Lorsch 1986). While most of these new trends—and the literature that describes them—refer to the corporate world, some analysts believe they constitute a model for such unlikely candidates as university organizations in the postindustrial world (Dill and Sporn 1996).

I believe we should not be swept away by either corporate or scholarly enthusiasts who believe that the days of organizational hierarchy are numbered and that in the interests of efficiency, the infrastructure of economic and other organizational life will be supplanted by a mix of market, monitoring, network, coordinating, and individual self-regulating mechanisms. However, it seems clear that we may expect a major reconceptualization of received notions of division of labor, hierarchy, commitment, and incentives in light of ongoing changes in organizations in postindustrial society.

Social Movements

Social movements lie at the meso level of social organization because they are phenomena to which individuals forge direct ties as participants, in which they interact directly with others, through which they seek to realize their collective aims and effect changes in their social environment, and in which, as meaningful points of social reference, they often find personal identities as well as day-by-day rhythms in their lives.

It is instructive to call to mind some features of the history of the sociological study of social movements. In the nineteenth century macrosociological theorists—notably Marx and Tocqueville—recognized revolutionary movements as an integral part of convulsive historical change. But the social psychology and sociology of social movements began properly with the work of Gustav Le Bon, the French journalist, toward the end of the nineteenth century. Le Bon's ([1895] 1952) analysis was irrationalist in the extreme, treating crowds as unreasoning, impulsive, emotional, swayed by suggestion and demagoguery, dissolving individuals' self-control, and capable of the most extreme destructiveness and idealism. Furthermore, he abhorred the crowd as destructive of institutions, and attributed the rise of the "era of crowds" to a pathology unleashed by the decay of traditional feudal and religious institutions.

Le Bon's social psychology dominated the field for some decades, providing the major underpinnings of the psychological theories of Sigmund Freud ([1922] 1955), William MacDougall (1920), and the American sociologist E. A. Ross (1916). By the middle of the twentieth century this irrationalist and negative assessment of collective behavior was attenuated, as these phenomena became the object of what may be called "naturalistic" inquiry, that is, as the object of scientific inquiry and "to be explained" as a matter of scientific interest. Investigators like Herbert Blumer (1951) dealt primarily with the mechanisms involved (e.g., milling), Ralph Turner and Lewis Killian (1957) considered processes by which groups came to define their situation and develop normative understandings, and my own work (Smelser 1962) dealt with the ideologies guiding collective behavior and social movements and identified a diversity of social conditions—including macrosociological structures—that operate as determinants in the development of social movements. In this process the dominant imagery of collective behavior and social movements as "irrational" and "threatening" receded in favor of a certain attitude of dispassion.

In the 1960s, a decade notable for the proliferation of social movements (the civil rights, student, antiwar, feminist, and countercultural movements, for example), the literature on social movements took a dramatic turn. For one thing, advocates of and sympathizers with those movements were among those who contributed to the literature, and they understandably regarded them as setting the world right and thus as far from irrational and threatening. One extreme statement (Skolnick 1969) treated the movements of the day as fundamentally rational, that is, as containing a *correct* diagnosis of the ills of contemporary society, and treated authorities and others who opposed the movements as irrational in their defense of a corrupt and unjust status quo. In accord with this orientation, contributors to this literature tended to regard all past theories of social movements as "irrationalist," conservative, and apologetic for one establishment or another.

Since the 1960s two main lines of analysis have come to dominate the study of social movements. The first is "resource mobilization theory." It crystallized in the work of scholars such as Meyer Zald and Roberta Asch (1966) and William Gamson (1975). Its basic theoretical thrust is that social movements are not to be explained by the recruitment of the alienated and the disaffected to irrational or nonrational "ideologies." In that respect the resource mobilization approach resembled the view that rose in the 1960s. Instead, social movements are better regarded as purposive, directed enterprises whose success or failure depends on their effectiveness in mobilizing resources (financial support, existing groups, and recognition by political parties, for example). It is apparent that this kind of interest in social movements marked a turn in a "rationalist" direction, even though resource mobilization analysts tend to maintain a neutral stance with respect to the larger social significance of social movements in society. This theoretical orientation also led to a focus on social movement organizations (SMOs), those organized groups that make it their business to mobilize resources on behalf of the movement. By this circumstance the study of social movements moved closer to—and, in a certain sense, became part of—the study of formal organizations, those special organizations dedicated to mobilizing resources, holding adherents' loyalties, and gaining political successes for the movement. That focus excited, in turn, the study of strategy, tactics, and decision making. That framework continues to dominate the literature on social movements, though it also has come in for its share of criticism for downplaying the ideological, social psychological, and cultural aspects of movements. A revived interest in the role of ideas and ideology has developed around the idea of "framing," or the active efforts on the part of social movement organizations and actors to produce and maintain "meaning for constituents, antagonists, and bystanders or observers" (Snow and Benford 1992).

The second development, largely European in origin and interest, is called "new social movements." Its starting point was the recognition by European intellectuals and social scientists that "old social movements"—working-class union and revolutionary movements understandable in the context of a Marxian worldview—were by and large spent, as was the Marxian analysis of society. The "new" social movements were not especially class based; included among them were regional, racial-ethnic, and language movements; antiwar and antinuclear movements; the feminist movement; and various countercultural and lifestyle movements. Most interpreters of the new social movements retained a neo-Marxist or neocritical note in their explanations, however, in that they interpreted those movements as a kind of generalized protest against an oppressive capitalist-state-bureaucratic-technological-media complex in postmodern society. The new social movements impulse has diminished in the past decade, and although those who wrote in that tradition accurately described a historical change in the pattern of social movements, their literature can best be understood as a dialogue among those interested in the Marxist and critical traditions of sociology.

This brief review of the sociological study of social movements is of some interest in itself, but for present purposes, I include it because it throws light on three problematics in sociology as a discipline, as follows:

- At the meso as well as the micro level the problem of assigning motives, reasons, and understandings to the people and the organizations we study is a recurrent methodological concern. Le Bon and those he influenced faced the concern directly, by endowing participants in social movements with irrationality, if not derangement; those who single out the alienated or the estranged as candidates for social movements also have a "theory" of why certain social circumstances predispose individuals to be attracted to ideologies of social movements; and even those resource mobilization theorists who tend to regard motivation as secondary have not been able to escape the issue of why people are predisposed to being mobilized. The problem of understanding "other minds" thus manifests itself at analytic levels higher than that of social psychology and social interaction.

- The history of the study of social movements underscores a special vulnerability of sociology in general—how difficult it is, when studying a subject matter of charged moral and political significance, to maintain a posture of neutrality and dispassion toward it. Many of the scholars mentioned had no hesitation about evaluating their subject matter. Perhaps more significant, even when a scholar makes a good faith effort to remain neutral about dramatic and publicly controversial phenomena, others in subsequent generations will locate some bias—real or imagined—no matter how successful or unsuccessful that scholar was in his or her own scientific intentions.

- This tradition of study also underscores the difficulty that social scientists have in coming to terms with the nonrational aspects of social life. They find them difficult to formalize theoretically, so they are forever being consigned to some kind of residual status. Or, alternatively, social scientists give in to the temptation to make rational that which, on its face, is not. I regard these tendencies as occupational hazards facing social scientists. After all, all of us are intellectuals and trained professionals, and the major institutional commitment in those universities and colleges in which we have been formed is still to the pursuit of the truth, which means the pursuit of the rational. Especially in the late twentieth century, when the nonrational impulses I have documented are in full sway, we are still prone to interpret the world in our own rationalist image. It would behoove us to engage in a campaign of self-examination to recognize and perhaps break ourselves of that tendency.

This last point leads me to identify a paradox in our contemporary situation as social scientists. It is evident that the resource mobilization and related approaches to the study of social movements are of a rationalist stripe (i.e., calculative, purposive, understandable-in-our-terms). They have more or less consigned the nonrational to a position of residuality or nonstudy, despite the minor comeback of interest in ideology in the resource mobilization literature. At the same time, the late twentieth century has produced a range of social movements—roughly speaking, those identified in the literature on the new social movements—that possess elements that are not readily understandable, or if understandable only by stretching, in terms of our dominant conceptions of rationality. The evidence of absolute ideologies, commitment without apparent calculation as well as primordial imagery and behavior, stands out in many social movements of our time. Does it not strike you as odd—as it strikes me—that we as social scientists interested in social movements should, in the late twentieth century, be so preoccupied with the rational aspects of social movements, precisely when the nonrational elements are so self-evident? I remind you that what I have just noted is a *general* problematic that has and will run through these essays: to take cognizance of the nonrational in social life, to recognize it as such, and to take it as deserving substantial attention in our enterprise.

Institutions

As we consider institutions, we begin to stretch the limits of the meso level. I regard institutions as lying at the core of social structure, and social structure belongs—as the next chapter will show—at the level of the macro. For that reason I will make only two observations about institutions, both of which touch the meso level, reserving the fuller discussion of social structure until later. By institutions I understand those complexes of roles, normative systems, and legitimizing values that constitute a functionally defined set of activities that gain permanence through the very processes of institutionalization. A concrete listing of institutions reveals a conventional inventory: family, education, religion, medicine, science, business, law, government, and others.

My first point is that institutions—structures at a general level of societal organization—are in large part "imagined," much as societies themselves are imagined communities (Anderson 1983). This means that they are not "seen" in any immediate sense, in the way that neighbors, policemen on the beat, the corner grocery store, and the local school are seen. At the same time, these institutions are "public," in the sense that they appear as nouns in language, and are spoken of as if they enjoy an empirical existence—as implied, for example, in the question, What is happening to education these days? This simultaneous invisibility ("imaginedness") and reality means that the *agents* or *spokespersons* who represent the institution assume a special sociological significance. With regard to the family as an institution, for example, these agents are vocal parents, psychologists and psychiatrists, educators, social workers, advocates for "family values," and others, including sociologists. They speak for, define, and represent the institution in the public and political arenas. These processes of representation are not well understood and merit understanding. They link the institution with the microworld of individual understanding and the macroworld of politics and public policy.

By the same token, individual persons do not interact with "institutions" per se, but with persons who represent the institution in day-by-day interaction. These representatives and their interactions shape institutions as well, but in ways different from those of the public spokespersons working on their behalf. These persons—lawyers, teachers, physicians, and so on—also hold the fate of the institution in their hands, because they are the ones who put forward the day-by-day presence of it and define, correct, modify, or reinforce the "folk" understandings of the institutions. This aspect of institution representing also deserves more systematic study.

TWO POINTS IN CONCLUSION

I have already moved into the supraindividual world in this chapter, and I will move even further in the chapters to come. This raises a long-standing question in sociology, that of the "group mind" or of "supraindividual" levels of reality. I do not wish to enter into all the ranges of controversies and misunderstandings that have surrounded these issues over time, but to make only one comment. At a certain point in the study of characteristics, attitudes, and behavior, we must turn to the involvement of individuals in higher levels of social organization—meso, macro, and global—that constitute a clear set of determinants. We may or may not want to describe these levels as *real* in some epistemological sense, but to proceed without taking into account the constraints of higher levels of social organization is to fail as sociologists.

On an entirely different note, let me suggest that in the contemporary world we face what might be described as a crisis at the meso level of social organization. Why should this be a crisis? On the one hand, the advanced nations of the world confront a situation in which the historically important meso levels of social integration—the immediate family, the extended family, the community, the neighborhood, the church, the tavern, the club, and, more recently, the political party—have declined and are continuing to decline in their significance as mechanisms of social integration. This decline is undeniable. At the same time, those social forms that might be regarded as taking their place—the fissions and fusions, the situationally based groups, the formal organizations, the social movements, for example—either have not done so or are in such a stage of transition that they cannot be considered to be adequate functional substitutes. We might then ask: Where is the meso in contemporary society, and where is it going?

That question looks both downward and upward. We know that mesostructures are important from the standpoint of the psychological continuity and identity of individual persons. What is the future of the person if we do not know the nature of the mesostructures in which the person is involved? Also, we know that the mesostructures—the heart and soul of our civil society—affect the character and effectiveness of the social integration of the larger society. To pose this question is not to answer it. But, speaking as a sociologist, I have to say that if we do not keep our eye on the meso level, we are likely to ignore the most problematic feature of society of the coming decades.

CHAPTER THREE

Macrosociology

The term "macrosociology" brings immediately to mind the idea of society, that social apparatus that has long been an ultimate point of reference in the organization of social life. Or so it seems. I begin this chapter with the observation that the idea of society is itself problematic—and is becoming more so all the time. I will close on the same note, and this will lead us naturally to the topic of the final chapter, the suprasocietal or global level.

THE CENTRAL PLACE OF THE NATIONAL SOCIETY IN THE SOCIAL SCIENCES

Virtually all of the social sciences, themselves children of the nineteenth- and twentieth-century domination of the nation-state, have, in one way or another, taken a version of that entity as the framing context for their respective intellectual enterprises. Consider the following:

- For political science, the nation, the state, and the national government and its institutions have constituted the fundamental basis of study.

- For economics, the basic macroeconomic unit has been the national economy. Writing only two decades ago, Simon Kuznets

(1972: 1–2) stated that nation-states set the "institutional bound-aries within which markets operate and within which human resources are relatively free to handle material capital assets and claims to them." Most analyses of international trade have dealt with interaction among national units.

- For sociology, the corresponding unit has been the national society, the seat of social integration and social institutions. The notion of society, moreover, involves a confluence of self-sufficiency, political integrity, social solidarity, and cultural identity.

- For cultural and social anthropology, the prime unit has been the "culture," stressing commonality of values, language, beliefs, and sense of identity but not necessarily having the attributes of a nation. This circumstance probably derives from the fact that many of the units studied by anthropologists have not been nations but rather tribal and other subnational groups. However, the concept of culture has proved easily translatable into the idea of a "national culture," as in references to German, Japanese, or American culture.

In this chapter and the next I will wonder about the continuing viability of this focus. But for the moment let us review some of the characteristics assigned to that favored unit.

The modern national society, or state, was consolidated in the intellectual and ideological work of writers like Thomas Paine and in the political and social work of the French Revolution. The composite view of the national state that emerged from that work was an identifiable social apparatus that *fused* a remarkable number of features of organized social life: geographic boundedness, political sovereignty, monopoly of force and violence by military and police forces, economic self-sufficiency, cultural integration or solidarity, a common language, and the political identity of a citizenry.

To give several examples of this emphasis: Society as the basic organizing unit found expression in Durkheim's first work, which dealt with the division of labor *in society* ([1893] 1984). His primary conceptual unit was the society. That body, consistently regarded as a kind of organism, possesses an organic integrity. Intersocietal relations were not especially problematical for him, nor were subsocieties. In Durkheim's analysis of differentiation, he consistently spoke of segmentary and complex *societies*. Also, his treatments of the division of economic labor, the differentiation of political, administrative, and judicial functions (ibid., 1–2), and the differentiation of social institutions such as the family (ibid., xlv) were significant mainly at the *societal level*. Integration, too, is a societal phenomenon; mechanical solidarity is an attribute of undifferentiated *societies,* and organic solidarity an attribute of complex *societies.* With respect to the latter, Durkheim recognized the significance of subsocietal bases of solidarity but regarded them as on the wane. Thus:

> [In peasant societies], . . . since economic activity has no repercussions outside the home, the family suffices to regulate it. . . . But this is no longer so when trades develop. . . . [I]f domestic society is no longer to play this [regulatory, integrative] role, another social organ must indeed replace it in order to exercise this most necessary function. (Ibid., xlv–vi)

> If there is one truth that history has incontrovertibly settled, it is that religion extends over an ever-diminishing area of social life. (Ibid., 119)

> Gradually [local customs] merge into one another and unify, at the same time as dialects and patois dissolve into a single national language and regional administration loses its autonomy. (Ibid., 136)

The replacement for these declining functions was found in an assertion of the society itself; "the more we evolve, the more societies develop profound feeling of themselves and their unity" (ibid., 123). For Durkheim, the society frames all that is social.

This comprehensive view of the national society survived in the functionalist and other traditions of modern sociology. In his work on comparative sociology, Robert Marsh (1967: 10) defined a society as having the following characteristics: "(1) a definite territory; (2) recruitment in large part by sexual reproduction; (3) a comprehensive culture; that is, cultural patterns sufficiently diversified to enable the members of the society to fulfill all the requirements of social life; (4) 'political' independence; that is, a society is not a subsystem of any other system, except in a very partial sense." About the same time Parsons (1966: 9) defined a society as "a type of social system . . . which attains the highest level of self-sufficiency as a system in relation to its environments." These "environments" included the definition of ultimate reality, cultural systems, personality, behavioral organism, and the physical-organic environment—in relation to which the society was a self-sufficient, integrating, and coordinating agency.

This "strong" and "closed" notion of the national society was a product not only of the intellectual efforts of social theorists and social scientists. It also emerged from the more or less organized projects of modern national societies themselves, which, in their recent histories, have pursued policies of securing the monopoly of force and violence in the national state; cultural integration through schooling, language policies, and the media; and loyalty and identification by cultivating and appealing to nationalistic sentiments. In a word, national societies themselves have worked toward that fusion, or unity of national economy, polity, society, and culture—to make the "imagined communities" (Anderson 1983) of modern national societies into real communities.

In this chapter and the next I will take a double line of attack. On the one hand, I will recognize the continuing validity of the national society by discussing some of its own problematics; on the other, I will argue that the notion of the national society is coming into question, both as an empirical entity and as a core organizing construct in the social sciences.

ONGOING PROBLEMATICS
OF CONTEMPORARY SOCIETIES

It is my impression that the concept of social structure—as well as the allied concepts of institution and role—has experienced a loss of status in sociological thinking in the past several decades (for a similar observation, see Eisenstadt 1995: 19–20). If this impression is correct, three intellectual developments might be cited as partially responsible for the decline. The first was the assault on structural-functional analysis—to which both institution and role were central—in the 1960s and 1970s. The assault came mainly through the "microsociological revolution" of the period (which tended to treat those constructs as illegitimate reifications) and through the neo-Marxist and neo-Weberian ascendancy of the same period (which, however, retained social structure as a central organizing construct). The second was the subsequent assault on the Marxian perspective, stemming from both intellectual and political dissatisfactions with it. The third development was a revision of the notion of culture, earlier regarded mainly in its legitimizing role with respect to social structure but now increasingly conceived in its psychological significance ("identity"), its significance as "project" or "strategy," and its significance as an instrument of domination. In this chapter I try to right the balance and argue that a number of long-standing concerns with social structure do and should retain their traditional importance.

The Continuing Salience of Structural Differentiation

The notion of structural differentiation is a major thread of analysis in economics and sociology. That conception arises from the acknowledgment that the structured allocation of activities in society is variable and that a pivotal line of variation is the degree to which these activities are specialized, or *differentiated* from one another. Adam Smith ([1776] 1937) made the division of labor—the economic version of structural differentiation—central to his analysis of the causes of increased economic productivity and the resulting wealth of nations, as well as the organizing concept for his theory of international trade. Karl Marx ([1867] 1949), too, recognized that an increased division of labor is a fundamental force in competitive capitalism. The idea of differentiation lay at the heart of Herbert Spencer's (1897) theory of evolution, and although that special theory was rejected by Durkheim ([1893] 1984), the idea of structural differentiation (the social division of labor) remained as the key structural element in the evolution from segmental to complex societies. Differentiation is central to the sociology of Georg Simmel as well, and formed the cornerstone of his concern with the development of modern society. However, Simmel stressed not only the economic and social efficiency of differentiation but also its capacity to create individualism and individual freedom (see Dahme 1990). Simmel's insight found expression in Parsons's (1966) subsequent observation that structural differentiation is the main lever for freeing individuals from their traditional ascriptive ties.

Structural differentiation also lies at the center of Parsons's (1961, 1966) *general* theory of social change, is a central theme in one strand of modernization theory (e.g., Smelser 1964), is a recurring theme in my own work (Smelser 1959, 1991), finds a significant place in the theoretical work of Luhmann (1982), and survives in "neofunctionalist" theory (Alexander and Colomy 1990). In most of these manifestations, differentiation appears as a description of and mechanism for the transition from traditional to modern social structure and, in that connection, carries an explicitly or implicitly adaptive—even evolutionary—connotation of the increasing rationalization and efficiency of social life.

Even though we have presumably moved from the "modern" to a "postmodern" phase of civilization, differentiation remains a commanding feature of a contemporary society. The continuing proliferation of specialized occupations (especially in the service sector) and the continuing march of bureaucratic organizations give witness to the process, as does the dramatic increase in the international specialization of production. Nor is the phenomenon restricted to economic and administrative activities. The rise of the modern nuclear family involved a differentiation of economic activity away from the family by relocating work in factories and other formal organizations, leaving the family a more focused unit, "specializing" in socialization and intimacy. Also, the eclipse of arranged marriage and the rise of romantic love as the basis for marriage marked a differentiation of courtship both from kinship and from the transmission of property and status. In the contemporary world we witness a radical extension of that process. The increase in numbers and legitimacy of the nonconjugal household, the single-parent household, homosexual cohabitation, and communal living signifies, among other things, a differentiation and dispersion of the nuclear family's previous monopoly on intimacy to other kinds of relationships. Similarly, the establishment of nursery school, preschool, day care, play group, and other collective arrangements is a differentiation of socialization in the early years, with the family's previous near-monopoly once again dispersed. To choose a final example, one of the political aims of feminism has been to differentiate gender identification from occupational and status placement.

As indicated, the idea of structural differentiation has had an affinity with theories of progress and social efficiency, though that emphasis has weakened recently. While that dimension continues to be relevant, it constitutes only one aspect of the process. The following additional problematics are associated with the idea of differentiation.

- More attention should be directed toward the *inefficiencies* and other costs associated with increased differentiation. Two traditions of research have this emphasis—first, the literature on diminished psychological gratification, increased alienation, and anomie associated with specialized roles; and second, the literature on inefficiencies (such as indecision, red tape, subversion of goals) associated with bureaucratization. Still other lines of inquiry are in order. To mention only one, while it is apparent that collective arrangements for the socialization of very young children are "efficient" in that they free parents for participation in the market and other activities, less is known about the psychic benefits and costs of placing so much socialization in the hands of professionals and other nonfamily agents.

• The presumed causes of differentiation should be expanded beyond the more or less rational, often post facto assumption that social structures differentiate in order to augment social efficiency. I have in mind, as an example, the notion of structural differentiation as *response to political conflict*. Years ago Michel Crozier (1964) interpreted the proliferation of bureaucratic rules as an accumulation of responses to conflict situations so that similar conflicts either would not recur or, if they did, could be "handled" by the new machinery. Similarly, the proliferation of regulative and watchdog agencies to guard against conflicts of interest constitutes a differentiation of structural forms to deal with political and ethical problems and conflict. One may call this "efficiency" if one wishes, but that stretches the term and does not pinpoint the political process involved.

• Because of the explicit or implicit linkage of differentiation with efficiency or progress, models of the process (e.g., Smelser 1959) tended to focus on *successful* differentiation, that is, sequences that actually produced more differentiated structures and more complex arrangements. Empirically, however, that process is not smooth, largely because differentiation involves the modification or even eradication of existing arrangements and often displaces incumbents of existing roles (as in technological unemployment). This means that efforts to change encounter corresponding counterpressures, usually in the form of vested interests. A frequent result is "blocked differentiation"—a kind of social paralysis as pressures to change build but yield chronic group conflict rather than structural change. In my study of the rise of state-supported education for the working classes in nineteenth-century Britain (Smelser 1991), I found it less profitable to regard the process as one of orderly differentiation than to treat it as a prolonged paralysis, with evident pressures to establish schooling for the working-class young (mainly concerns with pauperism and social order) being stalled for long periods by unresolvable conflicts among religious groups interested in promoting *their kind* of education.

- In the first instance, differentiation produces changes in the social structure. Yet the results of differentiation also shape the structuring of groups, group interests, and group conflicts and in that way spill over directly into the political process. The story often unfolds in the following way. The differentiation of a new structure creates positions (or roles) that are occupied by new incumbents. Industrial development, for example, produces manual workers with various levels of skill, supervisors, engineers, sales personnel, and the like. An advanced medical system produces doctors, nurses, technicians, hospital administrators, and more. Incumbency in these roles, moreover, becomes the basis for common *interests* of incumbents, and for the formation of groups (mainly unions and associations) that may assume significance as conflict groups. Putting these ingredients together, we produce the following abstract model of process.

differentiation → categorization → social group →

consciousness of group → political mobilization → social change

This kind of model informed Marx's ideas linking the economic and political processes. As the result of capitalist development (differentiation) a class of propertyless wage earners (category) is created; then, through mutual contact and communication, this category becomes a group with definite consciousness of its situation and on the basis of this consciousness becomes a politically active group that ultimately overthrows the system.

Marx regarded these transitions as more or less inevitable within capitalist development. But as subsequent history has demonstrated, the transitions from social categories to groups with consciousness to political action groups are problematical rather than inevitable. Some social categories (roles) become the basis for groups and others do not; moreover, category-based groups that do not have consciousness at one moment gain it at another—particularly when they are threatened in some way. Furthermore, processes of differentiation can work to divide groups as well as unite them. More than one observer (Mills 1951; Dahrendorf 1959) has pointed out that the proliferation of multiple work roles, and especially service (white- and pink-collar) roles has worked to subvert Marx's prediction that a propertyless proletariat *as a whole* would develop common class consciousness and become a directed conflict group.

One key agenda item for sociologists, then, is to link social structure (i.e., the kaleidoscope created by processes of structural differentiation) and group life in society by generating models and conducting empirical investigations that focus on the determinants of the contingent transitions among social structure, social categories, social groups, group consciousness, and group action.

The Increasing Salience of Diversity

The idea of differentiation concerns above all roles and institutions that have *functional* significance. It tells us a great deal, moreover, about groups and group conflicts precipitated from the panoply of structured roles. Crosscutting these functional roles, however, is another range of social categorizations, both ascribed and self-assigned, that also constitute bases for assignment to functional roles, personal and group identification, prejudice and discrimination, and the political process. Among ascribed categories are race, ethnic membership, native language, region or locality, age, gender, and religion (the latter a mixed category, because religion often involves a mixture of ascription and personal choice). Among nonascribed bases are membership in social movements, some based on the ascriptions mentioned—as in the case of feminism and regional political groups—but some issue based, as in the case of the peace movement, the environmental movement, the animal rights movement, and other groupings based on cultural choice, such as lifestyle and counterculture. Sometimes these categories overlap with functional structures—when women are assigned to certain occupations or to greater responsibility for child care in the family, or when occupations are segregated by race (slavery is the extreme case). Despite this overlap, a distinction can be made between functionally differentiated roles and these other social categories. The former describe the *differentiation* of society, the latter its *diversity*. Even this distinction is not a clean one, because part of the cultural diversity of modern societies arises from distinctive cultural groupings derived from functionally based groups (e.g., working-class culture, peasant culture, and yuppie lifestyle).

The social bases of diversity are historically variable. Long periods of Western history have been marked by the salience of *religious* diversity, though this has declined since the rise of industrialism and nationalism. (We cannot forget, however, the residual religious basis of some European political parties, and the continuing and extreme salience of religion in such areas as Northern Ireland, Lebanon, Syria, the former Yugoslavia and other Balkan areas, as well as fundamentalist movements everywhere.) Race as a biological category rose in salience during previous episodes of internationalization, especially enforced slavery and colonization. Before the onset of industrial-market and national bases of organization, locality and local culture served as the primary basis of social interaction and identification. This basis has withstood the institutional and sometimes-conscious political efforts of the market and nation-state to displace it, and in the past decades localism—expressed in terms of demands for autonomy, integrity, and recognition—has reasserted itself. In fact, the social bases of race ethnicity, language, gender, sexual preference, and to some extent age have come forward as salient bases of group identification and politics—so as to give life to labels such as "cultural diversification," "multiculturalism," "the new tribalism," and "identity politics." These developments have been as dramatic as they were difficult to predict. Whether or how long they will persist is uncertain and equally difficult to predict.

We do not understand the reasons for the resurgence of these kinds of diversity, but any ultimate explanation will have to take account of at least the following factors.

- Certain categories have become more salient largely by virtue of realistic demographic and economic changes. For example, long-term demographic trends—mainly reduced fertility and mortality—have led to dramatic increases in the numbers (and therefore political significance) of the elderly in developed societies. The institutionalization of retirement has also given clearer visibility and commonality of experience as a category removed from the active labor force. Furthermore, the mobilization of the elderly on their own behalf has raised the political consciousness of *other* age groups, especially in relation to taxation and welfare issues. In addition, the mobilization and political significance of the feminist movement cannot begin to be understood apart from the dramatically increased—but in many respects still disadvantaged—participation of women in the paid labor force since World War II, which created new interests and new consciousness among women.

- In many respects cultural diversification has resulted from an actual diversification of populations in many nations through international, interregional, and intranational movement of peoples. This, in turn, has resulted from changes in demand for labor (e.g., guest workers), from wars and other political crises that have produced migrant populations, and from increased tourism. There seems to be no reason to believe that such movements will not increase.

- The political dynamics of localities—both urban and nonurban—generate polarization between "newcomers" and "natives." These dynamics are overdetermined by several subprocesses— the tendencies for newcomers simultaneously to compete economically and to self-segregate culturally, both of which add to their visibility and their threat; the tendencies for natives to react defensively to preserve economic positions, political power, and ways of life; and the interaction of these two tendencies to produce cultural and political polarizations.

- The most common verdict on the role of the media, especially television, is that they are culturally homogenizing, and their spread through the whole world is cited in support of this. The effects are, however, evidently more complex. Television brings cosmopolitan reality to localities, thus "diversifying" them, at least during that long and never-completed transition to cosmopolitanism. Similarly, the international presence of the media— to be discussed more in the final chapter—diversifies, and never completely conquers the developing world. Moreover, the media, particularly in the United States, tend to "tame" diversity by including it explicitly in programming and advertising, thus elevating issues such as race, gender, and sexual preference to greater salience for the *general* viewing public and imparting greater "diversity" of exposure to their audiences.

- Presently I will lay out a number of reasons why it is difficult for polities—especially democratic ones—to deal with political groups that present their demands in cultural terms. In fact, there is evidence that polities often conspire in the unsuccessful attempt to downplay the political salience of categories such as race, ethnicity, gender, and sexual preference. However, the realities of politics sooner or later force them to recognize these groups as political entities in their own right, and when they do, they tend to heighten the political significance of those categories. The United States is a telling example. Largely as a result of the civil rights and feminist revolutions stretching from the late 1950s into the 1970s, federal and state governments came explicitly and officially to acknowledge the political presence of these groups, largely in the form of programs under the heading of "affirmative action." In doing so they *made visible* race and gender as political categories with a certain presumption to political entitlement, even as they denied that employment practices constituted favoritism and rejected the idea of quotas based on race and gender. And in doing that, they have conveyed the message that entitlement-like demands on the part of ethnic, sexual preference, physically disabled, and other groups were fair game in politics and, over time, have been greeted with similar political demands on the part of Native Americans, Asian Americans, Latino Americans, gay groups, and, not least, "white ethnics" and, to a lesser degree, white males in general. The recent efforts on the part of aspiring Republican politicians and others to diminish or abolish affirmative action can be understood as a response both to this backlash and to the difficulties created by ascriptive politics.

- The combined effect of the internationalization of the economy (with a corresponding loss of control of nation-states over their economic fortunes) and the development of regional political alliances (such as the European Union and, to a lesser degree, North America) has no doubt given advantage to subnational regional, ethnic, and language movements in their programs to lay claim to political loyalty. And, again paradoxically, as these very movements gain momentum and legitimacy, they become active forces in the weakening of the nation-state as an object of loyalty and a focus of cultural identity.

- It has been suggested that the tendencies to localization, including the dissolution of former empires and states, are, in fact, a *protest* against the growing scope of world markets and global politics, perhaps even some kind of reassertion of the limits on human bonding, which cannot extend itself indefinitely in scope, superficiality, and diversity. This argument, while worth considering, is very difficult to demonstrate, and is perhaps beyond proof. However, it does make sense to interpret the reassertion of localism and local autonomy as an effort on the part of human groups to gain control in a world that appears to be becoming increasingly uncontrollable.

These diverse factors constitute a helter-skelter list of plausibles; they do not provide anything like a full explanation. What is clear, however, is that the combination of accelerating differentiation *and* increasing diversification in contemporary societies has also changed the fundamental terms of two additional sociological dimensions: stratification and integration. To these phenomena we now turn.

The Changing Face of Stratification

There was a time in the recent history of sociology when two perspectives of social stratification held dominant positions. The first, the functional, proposed that a combination of occupational status and level of education operated as the prime determinants of social ranking in society—this ranking traceable, in turn, to the cultural values of industrial society. One subtradition of research, noting similarities of prestige rankings in most societies studied, held this kind of ranking to transcend both political systems and traditional cultural values (Treiman 1977). The second, the Marxist, tied social stratification to property relations in the capitalist system; this approach focused less on ranking than on class and class conflict. The approaches resembled one another, however, in that each inextricably linked inequality with the dictates of modern industrial society, though the approaches differed in the particulars of diagnosis, explanation, and political flavor. In the 1990s both systems retain some relevance to the realities of social organization, but both seem increasingly out of date, for reasons I will now explore.

A corollary of both perspectives—functionalist explicitly and Marxist implicitly—was that the *unit* of the stratification system was the nuclear family household and that the main agent in that household was the male job- or occupation-holder. For functional analysts in particular, the social ranking of the kinship unit depended on a mix of the occupational role (primary), education, and income of the husband-father. The neatness of that view of the stratification system has become more and more muddled in recent decades, in large part because of the following kinds of changes.

- The universal basis of economic, occupational activity for social status has come in for repeated questioning and criticism in various quarters: formulations by some economists that people prefer leisure over work; the repeated assertion that the United States has moved historically from a production-oriented to a consumption-oriented society; debates in Germany about the "uncoupling" of work and social status; glimmerings of such debates in Japan; and the apparent nostalgia of postsocialist societies for the "welfare and security" aspects of the socialist era, while at the same time renouncing its politically repressive aspects and desiring some sort of market-based economy with its promise of greater prosperity and higher levels of consumption. This is not the place to evaluate the validity of these assessments; but insofar as they tend to dethrone the relationship between work and social status, they raise questions about the criteria to be invoked in assessing the ranking systems of societies.

- The bases for assigning social rank have evolved to a new point of complexity and uncertainty. Increasing differentiation and numbers of occupations and jobs has yielded a less definite basis of ranking, if for no other reason than sheer multiplication. The simplicity of distinctions between—and translations into class terms of—manual and nonmanual labor, bourgeoisie and working class, and others, has become clouded in the light of the multiplication of occupations, especially in the service sector. Insofar as proletarianization has proceeded, further, it has not been as a form of manual labor but as a service proletariat, including low-wage clerical workers, fast-food workers, paid security personnel, and "temporary" workers of many descriptions. Interestingly, too, a new form of "duality" has appeared in labor markets; technological changes, foreign competition, and migration have created an unemployed surplus of low-skill workers. These workers, along with those who are hired on a periodic or part-time basis so as to avoid benefit payments (now as much as one-quarter of the American labor force, and growing), constitute an important segment of the lower-income population. Finally, the continuing embourgoisement of skilled workers, and their political alliances with some managers and owners on many issues dealing with free trade and protection, has blurred that classic division between labor and capital as well.

- Insofar as there was validity in the claim that women's status was determined primarily by the occupational and educational status of their husbands, that claim has now been weakened. The main challenge is the increased representation of women in the labor force and their partial entry into high-status managerial and professional positions that endow *them* with the social status connected with those positions—if they are married, sometimes independently of their husband's status, sometimes mingled with it. However, the status of women derived from occupation and education still presents ambiguities, partly because of traditional values and prejudices that do not cede full equity of evaluation for women and partly because of traditional assumptions—held by women as well as men—that women should *combine* an occupational career with childbearing and child-rearing responsibilities, which remain proportionately greater than the corresponding responsibilities of men. In a word, the long-term revolution in labor force participation by women has yielded a more complicated and less certain basis for social ranking.

- The traditional household itself—that is, husband and wife with children—has also been thrown into question by changes in the kinship structure. The major changes are high divorce rates, increases in single-person and single-parent households, increases in nonconjugal living arrangements, and increases in homosexual cohabitation. To assume that an ideal-type traditional household is the unit of stratification becomes, as a result, increasingly problematic.

- One of the infrequently recognized consequences of access of larger proportions of the population to higher education—evident in most developed societies—has also rendered education less certain as a determinant of status. General experience in higher education no longer constitutes a "ticket" to a high-status occupational position or a "credential" for social status. This is not to deny Bourdieu's emphasis on education as a source of cultural capital; rather, it is to agree with him that the opening of a previously elite avenue to status has become less valuable and less certain as a provider of that capital.

- Insofar as ascribed and quasi-ascribed bases of social organization assume greater salience, the more they are likely to be invoked in determining status and the more they cloud judgments about ranking and stratification. Put another way, diversification has become superimposed on differentiation as a basis for status, making both ranking and status identification more complex.

Most interpreters of the decline of class as an agency in the postmodern world—including both end-of-ideology theorists such as Daniel Bell and critical theorists such as Jürgen Habermas—have cited several factors: the increasing prosperity of the working classes, the politically calming effect of the institutionalized welfare state, and the incorporation of those classes into the political process via class-based political parties. Those diagnoses are true enough. I believe, however, that the points just enumerated lend an additional dimension of understanding. It has been not only a matter of *incorporating* a previously unincorporated political force into the polity; it has also been a matter of the progressive *diffusion* of class lines, so that the working class— or any other class, for that matter—has become less certainly identifiable, less conscious, and less mobilizable politically. These forces not only supplement the accounts given by postmodern theorists but also ramify the political process in other ways. They may, for instance, account not only for the relative weakening of class-based political parties; they may contribute to our understanding of the increasing salience of personality in political campaigns and our understanding of the increased reliance on media messages that are not specifically class messages. Furthermore, with the class and group structure of societies thus diffused, politicians themselves face a more ambiguous array of constituencies, mainly because familiar class lines of thinking match less well with social reality. Furthermore, the political salience of non-class-identified groups in the political process (ascribed groups and "new" social movements of various sorts) creates specific kinds of difficulties for the integration of society through the polity. To this last topic I now turn.

The Continuing Problematic of Societal Integration

In calling attention to social integration we must again begin with Durkheim, who more than any other scholar made that issue problematic. In doing so he was reacting in the first instance to the Spencerian notion, derived from Adam Smith's conception of the "invisible hand," that the individualistic pursuit of self-interest results in a *collective* or *societal* equilibrium that renders the issue of integration nonproblematic. For Durkheim, the answer could not be so simple. A more active, positive regulation was required. Durkheim found this mainly in the generation of a legal system that served to regulate the interdependencies of differentiated structures and agents. In addition, he gave the state a distinct and expanding integrative role: "There is above all one organ in regard to which our state of dependence continues to grow: this is the state. The points we come into contact with it are multiplied, as well as the occasions when it is charged with reminding us of the sentiment of our common solidarity" (Durkheim [1893] 1984: 173). Despite this acknowledgment, Durkheim himself, in effect, fashioned his own version of an automatic solution to the problem of solidarity: organic solidarity is found in and arises from the division of labor itself. His commitment to that notion lay behind his controversial proposition that anomie, class conflict, and other sources of instability are pathological and transitory.

Since Durkheim's time I believe that we, as sociologists, have revised his notions of solidarity in two fundamental ways. First, we have come to regard it as forever problematical and fragile, and forever requiring active efforts on the part of agents of integration to reproduce and sustain it in a national citizenry. Second, we have come to realize that there is not only one primary type of solidarity (organic solidarity) in complex societies but rather many types, and that these are related to and overlapping with but not reducible to one another. By way of a nonexhaustive identification, I list the following:

- Economic integration, or the interdependence of specialized economic agents via the market. This is the type of integration stressed by Adam Smith, which Durkheim criticized but at the same time acknowledged by placing differentiation so centrally in his own theory of integration.

- Political-legal integration, involving the role of government in the maintenance of social order through the regulation of behavior and the resolution of conflict.

- Cultural integration (including religion, common values, common ideology, and common language). This is the kind of integration associated with the writing of Talcott Parsons, who insisted, in perhaps his most controversial proposition, that all societies are characterized by a consensus on common, society-wide values.

- Integration through stratification-domination. Although this form bears a resemblance to political-legal domination, it is not the same. The premodern (and pre-nation-state) system of feudal "orders" is an example.

- Kinship integration, which binds persons related by blood, marriage, and adoption to one another. In some historical situations kinship is fused with stratification domination, as in the case of hereditary monarchy.

- Territorial integration, or the binding together of people by virtue of common residence and proximity.

As indicated at the outset, our sociological and political heritage has led us to expect that most of these aspects of integration are fused together in the modern nation-state—that is, the national economy, national territorial sovereignty, national monopolies over law, political regulation, and the means of violence, nationally based stratification systems, and national values or cultures.

The nub of the contemporary problem of both state and society, I would submit, is that this fusion at the societal level is by no means natural and that, in fact, we witness a growing *disjunction,* a systematic *moving apart,* of these bases of integration from one another and from the state and a corresponding *weakening* of the state as an integrative instrument. Let me only mention some salient evidence.

- The increasing regionalization and internationalization of production, finance, markets, and trade have carried the economic differentiation and integration more and more beyond the capacity of the state (Cable 1995).

- With the international movement of peoples, the augmentation of ascribed and semiascribed diversity within nations, and the survival of national minorities in newly founded states (conspicuously in the Balkans and in the former Soviet Union), the map of cultural solidarity coincides less and less with both territorial and national political integration (Brubaker 1995).

- With the diffusion of the mass media, as well as the technological possibilities for instantaneous invisible communication (via fax and the Internet) and encryption, national boundaries tend to dissolve. Furthermore, whatever control over the flow of information (including market transactions) national states previously enjoyed, is correspondingly weakened. These technological possibilities also suggest the possibility of internationally based informal economies that escape the notice of national authorities even more than national informal economies do.

Put in concise form, the major contradiction is that the nationally based systems of political-legal and territorial integration are being increasingly besieged by economic and political developments mainly "from above" and by cultural developments mainly "from below" the nation-state level. Those developments present a special problem for the vitality of political democracy. One of the hallmarks of that system of governance, as it has evolved, is that political authorities at the state (and often local) level are *elected by* and ultimately *accountable to* national electorates. But by virtue of the erosion of certain aspects of the state's integrative capacities, democratic representatives of national peoples become progressively less able to govern and assure integration, because they lose control of many of the fundamental instruments of integration. In a word, they are, more and more, being held accountable for matters for which they cannot be accountable.

One final issue concerning the governability of democratic societies traces to the phenomena of cultural diversification. Democratic theory has come to mean many things since its formulations by Plato and Aristotle, but one of those meanings with special contemporary relevance is the notion of democracy as a set of representative governmental institutions in a pluralistic society with diverse and competing interests. The effectiveness of those institutions, moreover, is assessed according to their ability to hear those interests, negotiate with those leaders who speak for them ("prolocutors," to use Mayhew's [1990] term), and forge compromises that, with varying degrees of success, are aimed at settling current and forestalling future conflicts.

This version of the democratic process is built on several primary presuppositions: that demands made on the polity are in principle amenable to compromise; that prolocutors and their groups can envision compromise as an outcome; and that those in government can, in principle, fashion compromises. A type of conflict that readily fits with these presuppositions is industrial disputes, in which management and labor come into conflict over the adjustment of wages and other conditions of work, and after a process of mediation or arbitration, some kind of mutually agreeable and binding, if not totally satisfactory, compromise position is put into place.

When claims on the polity do not meet these conditions, this creates difficulties for the democratic process. To choose another example from industrial relations, when conflicts between labor and management concern principles of *legitimacy,* or the right of unions to exist and to be heard, they take on an either-or, nonnegotiable character and make incremental give-and-take and compromise more difficult. To state the matter more generally, the demands made by value-based or culture-based groups (often primordial in character) prove difficult for politicians to deal with precisely because they tend to assume an absolute, nonnegotiable character. The idea of primordialism implies above all that groups are usually rooted in sacred principles of membership or value-commitments. Defining themselves as sacred, primordial groups, they present positions and demands under the cloak of absolute principles that tend to have a noncompromising quality about them. To assert this is to argue neither that primordial groups do not have or express real interests nor that they do not engage in compromises. It is to argue, however, that primordial groups fuse interest claims with first principles, and this makes the process of compromise more difficult.

It follows that politicians and bureaucrats—the agents of the polity—tend to find the political demands of primordial groups un-congenial. The reason for this is that they do not easily lend them-selves to compromise solutions that are the stock-in-trade of these agents. Consequently, when claims and conflicts of an absolute charac-ter arise, politicians in power tend to run for cover, to deny or other-wise minimize the primordial elements of those claims and conflicts, or to attempt to redefine them in ways that permit them to be dealt with as compromisable items. This is simply to assert that the increased salience of cultural diversification presents special challenges to demo-cratic polities because they press against the edges of the tacit "rules of the game" of democratic governance.

To raise these points about the fragility of national boundaries and the capacity of nation-states to integrate and govern leads us logically to the concerns of international or global sociology. The developments that influence the permeability and fragility of national boundaries and the capacity of nations to govern are, as indicated, intricately tied to developments in world society itself. We will face that society di-rectly in the final chapter, and note its characteristics and its capacity to penetrate national and local bases of social organization.

CHAPTER FOUR

Global Sociology

International sociology, or global sociology, which takes the relations among nations as its focus—or, alternatively, treats the world or some subsystem of it as its unit of analysis—is the least developed area of sociology. By now, however, it is one of the most important, largely because of the ongoing transformation of its subject matter, the world.

Most nineteenth-century European sociologists centered their attention on the developing Western world, the world in which they lived. They were interested mainly in deciphering—and alternatively celebrating or regretting—the sea of social changes that were revolutionizing the industrializing and democratizing world. The early American sociologists were similarly absorbed with the problems of their own industrializing, urbanizing, and diversifying society. Insofar as Western sociologists glanced abroad, they, along with their anthropological colleagues, did so through the lens of classical evolutionary analysis. These thinkers regarded most other societies as less developed than their own, and concentrated mainly on their differences from the more advanced West. And because they assumed that these societies stood, variably, somewhere along the line of evolutionary development—development believed to be either immanent or stemming from causes within society (e.g., technological forces)—they were not inclined to focus on the *relations* among nations.

While classical evolutionary theory was more or less thoroughly discredited by the early twentieth century, one aspect of it survived in the resurgent literature on modernization that dominated in the 1950s and 1960s. That was the recurrent focus on the *internal* dynamics of developing (and not-developing) societies—technology, entrepreneurship, investment, and the rural-to-urban transformation, as well as obstacles to modernization found in indigenous religions, kinship systems, and other ascriptive forms. As critics from the dependency and world system points of view were to argue subsequently, this inward focus constituted a systematic limitation and liability for that phase of modernization theory.

Sociology's neglect of the intersocietal does not, of course, tell the whole story. Without attempting to be exhaustive, I point to the following traditions of sociology with an international or global emphasis.

- In one respect Karl Marx was drawn away from the study of relations among societies, because, he, too, locked his analysis into an evolutionary scheme, dictated by stages of internal development of the forces and relations of production. At the same time, he clearly recognized the dynamic of capitalism as a quintessentially *international* phenomenon (Marx [1867] 1949) driven by its own contradictions and crises outside the boundaries of its own societies and spreading ultimately to the colonization, exploitation, and transformation of other regions of the world. Lenin ([1917] 1939) extended that principle in his formulation of imperialism as the last stage of capitalism, and insofar as world system theorists such as Immanuel Wallerstein (1974) adhere to the materialism derived from Marx, that tradition remains alive to this day.

- Another thread of internationalism appeared in the early twentieth century in the form of diffusionism in anthropology. Much of the impetus for the development of this approach arose from direct criticism of the "internalist" bias of classical evolutionary theory. Because culture traveled and was borrowed, diffusionists argued, societies could skip stages or otherwise alter the presumed fixity of developmental paths posited by the evolutionists. The early diffusionists, however, tended to concentrate on the migration of the cultural *items,* such as the calendar and the number zero, and they wrote little about the relations among societies, or the contextual modifications of items once borrowed. The diffusionist tradition is a continuing one. A later version of it appeared in the work of modernization theorists such as Alexander Gerschenkron (1962) and Reinhard Bendix ([1964] 1977), who regarded the modernization of latecomers to development as affected profoundly by their consciousness of, borrowing from, and competition with already-modernized nations.

- There is also a social science tradition of the study of colonial domination, with manifestations in anthropology, sociology, political science, economics, and history. This, too, has an internationalist flavor as well, since the study of colonialization inevitably excites an interest in the *relations* between colonial and colonized societies. A remarkable example is the last work of Bronislaw Malinowski (1945), which treated the transformation of British African colonies as a dialectical and synthetic process involving colonizing forces outside and traditional forces within. This tradition of colonial sociology, if we may call it that, continues among scholars in the West and in developing countries in their study of the past, as well as in their study of post- and neocolonial forms of domination.

- More recently, the perspectives of dependency and world system analysis, both spawned in part as reactions to the limitations of modernization theory, take the international economy and its patterns of domination as their starting point and trace the ramifications of that economy in the internal history of nations. While both these approaches have experienced their own season of criticism, and while adaptations of each have appeared, they have played an important role in generating the currently existing subfields of international and global sociology.

- We must also include reference to the tradition of systematic-comparative work, of which Weber's was foremost. Much of this tradition, however, treats similarities and differences among societies but not their relations to one another, and hence is not international in the sense I am using the term.

- One feature of international sociology is that it is scarcely sociology at all with respect to disciplinary concerns. Internationally minded economists, political scientists, sociologists, historians, and anthropologists deal with overlapping problems, and often approach these problems in an interdisciplinary way. Just as internationalization as a process is blurring the familiar boundaries of the world, so it is forcing social scientists to break down traditional disciplinary barriers among themselves.

THE NATURE OF CONTEMPORARY INTERNATIONALIZATION

So much for a sketch of some of the ways that social scientists have tried to comprehend the relations among nations and societies and to trace the influence of those relations on their internal structures and processes. The remainder of this chapter will be devoted to three lines of analysis: (1) to present the fundamental *directions* of change—and contradictions—on the current and future international scene; (2) to call attention to some sociological *dimensions* and *processes* involved in these changes; (3) to enunciate some *methodological* problematics that the study of international or global sociology raises.

I would identify four major ongoing revolutions in the world at the present time—some continuations of existing and known ones, some newer. Each revolution is interesting in its own right, but the *relation-*

ships among the four should command our attention especially. In these relations we will find notes of both unity and disunity.

The Continuing Revolution in Economic Growth

It is perhaps old-fashioned to point to economic growth as a revolution because we social scientists have recognized it, praised it, and—to some degree, at least—protested against its negative consequences for so long. But we must note it again because it has not abated. Indeed, it possesses all the momentum it ever had, and has taken on some new characteristics.

- The impetus to growth has diffused so much that the whole world aspires to it—the developed economic powers to protect their position, the newly industrializing countries to catch up, the Third World countries to break from their economic entrapment, and the world's economic and political leaders to preserve their positions of stability and profit. These are the loudest voices in the world today, and the power of those voices that speak otherwise is puny by comparison.

- The aegis for growth has been a resurgence of market-based capitalism with a heightened international character, involving the dramatic migration of production—most of the world's manufacturing is no longer located in the so-called industrial nations—and the accelerated international movement of all the factors of production. The major alternatives to capitalism—traditionalism, communism, socialism, and imaginative Third World forms—have collapsed or weakened, and some variant of capitalism has been embraced in their place. And on the global scene economic growth continues (irregularly and with stagnant periods), and international trade, markets, and finance spiral.

- The resurgence of world capitalism has many faces, but from a cultural point of view, it gives renewed priority to two features

of the human condition—*individual action* and *individual choice.*
First, there has been a resurgence of the free labor maket—the
trademark of which is incentives—in which employers and employees choose one another. Second, there has been an increase
in consumer markets in which the individual is regarded as capable of *choosing*—within his or her means—what goods and
services to purchase. Both these markets contrast with the traditional and administered systems of pricing, in which culture and
political authority, respectively, are the engines of exchange. To
point to this augmented formal freedom is by no means to ignore the fact that free labor and consumer markets often work
blindly, cruelly, and exploitatively—and thus create the paradox
of freedom in principle and lack of freedom in practice—but
none of this seems to have diminished their resurgence.

The Continuing Democratic Revolution

The second revolution is a political one, also an acceleration of a known
process. I refer to the continuing march of democracy and the democratic principle. Early in the nineteenth century Tocqueville ([1835]
1945) described the advance of democracy—with its facets of liberty
and equality—as a "providential fact," and nothing in subsequent history seems to have proved him wrong. The democratic impulse has
been one of the most vital during the past two centuries. The past
quarter-century, however, has witnessed what Samuel Huntington
(1991) called a "third wave" of democratization, beginning with the
revolutionary seizure in Portugal in 1974—a wave affecting dozens of
nations throughout the world and reaching a climax with the events
of Tiananmen Square in Beijing and surging through the former Soviet Union and the Eastern European countries.

While market-based capitalism and political democracy are distinct
phenomena, they resemble one another in one essential respect: both
give a high premium to the individual actor, individual choice, and in-

dividual agency. Political democracy celebrates active political participation, ennobles the individual citizen and voter, and presumably endows that individual with a measure of control over political affairs.

Needless to say, the dream of democracy has seldom, if ever, been realized in practice. Tendencies to stumble into political chaos or to backslide into authoritarian or totalitarian regimes are ever-present; electorates and citizens forever tend to fall into passivity; and critics remind us that formal democratic institutions often conceal other powerful processes of domination. Yet, in a way, these observations that democracy is forever on the verge of failure support the point: the *ideal* thrusts of that political system are agency, activism, and control, particularly when it is compared with its more traditionalistic and authoritarian alternatives.

The Revolution in Solidarity and Identity

The third great revolution is an *integrative* one. I referred to it in the last chapter while considering the fate of the modern nation-state. It is best described as a revolution in solidarity and identity. It is a reassertion of the salience of subnational *groups*. These may be based on region, religion, race, ethnicity, language, gender, lifestyle, or some mix of these. Alternatively, they may be solidary groups that are associated with *social movements* pressing for recognition, status, and rights of such groups, or advocating a cause such a peace or antagonism to nuclear power. This group impulse, traceable to the 1960s (Gurr 1994), appears everywhere in the world, though in different guises. Sociologists have noticed how successfully these groups compete with social class as a focus of organization and loyalty. They also tend to undermine *other,* traditional foci of subnational integration, such as organized religion, the community, the neighborhood, and kinship. During the past two centuries both industrial capitalism and the nation-state eroded these foci of integration. The newer integration based on different subnational solidarities has continued that war on those traditional forms by competing with them directly for the loyalty, affection, and commitment of individuals.

I noted that the acceleration of the market principle and the march of democracy share a premium on individual choice and agency. At first glimpse the increasing salience of new subnational solidary groups runs contrary to that theme. As often as not, membership in these groups comes close to what sociologists call *ascription*—the subordination of the individual to the group, whether because the individual is born into it or because it often demands an absolute commitment.

All this is true enough. But from another standpoint the vitalization of such groups is an *assertion* of human agency. Group leaders and members frequently represent themselves as solidary forces opposed to the nation-state—that invention which, I pointed out in the preceding chapter, fused territoriality, governance, identity, and group solidarity into a single entity. That fusion is now being challenged on every front. The challenging groups themselves provide, or promise to provide, a new basis for realizing human agency—if not individual in the first instance, then certainly collective—endowing their individual members with a sense of dignity, purpose, and action *through* the collectivity.

The Environmental Revolution

The fourth revolution, in varying strength throughout the world, is an environmental one. It is a kind of double revolution. The first arm involves the destruction of the natural world in which we live; the second arm involves the mobilization of consciousness, political activity, and policies designed to stem that destruction and establish some kind of "sustainable" equilibrium between humanity's domination of the natural world and its tendency to spoil, exhaust, or destroy it. The ravaging of the earth, its oceans, and its atmosphere is not new, but all signs point to the fact that it is increasingly massive and in the end constitutes the most important threat to humanity. Moreover, that threat is truly universal in character, because it involves the fate of the entire human species in relation to the sustaining environment—no respecter of nation, class, or group in its ultimate consequences, though its short-term effects are selective in these regards.

The second arm of the revolution, the environmental movement proper, is clearly in evidence, particularly in the developed countries of the world, but it is a weak force when compared to the threat itself. This relative weakness stems from two forces—first, the strength of the technological, economic, and demographic trends that are primarily responsible for environmental devastation, and second, the fragmentation of goals of the environmental movement (nuclear danger, water pollution, global warming, air pollution, toxification of the earth). Despite this, the environmental movement expresses the same impulse of human agency and activism that is found in the other three revolutions. That is to say, the environmental revolution acknowledges that only human beings can set right the balance between humanity and nature, just as human beings have been the agents who have threatened to ruin it.

Continuities and Contradictions among the Four Revolutions

I have identified one master impulse in all four revolutions. That impulse is *the insistence on behalf of individual agency, choice, and activism:* the ennoblement of human control of human affairs. This impulse has become more salient in the whole world, not only in the West where it was invented, defined, and cultivated. It manifests itself in all four of the revolutions, and in the largest sense makes the four into one. In recent years Alain Touraine (1991) has stressed above all the force of individualism in the modern world and traced its manifold benefits and costs to humankind. On the basis of the observations I have made, we can only underscore his message.

This commonality, however, is only a small part of the story. We cannot really imagine a unity among the four revolutions. The contemporary—and coming—world is fraught with old and new anomalies, paradoxes, and contradictions, both within each revolution and among them. Here are the most salient of these.

- We witness immediately one long-standing and familiar contradiction. The new and victorious surge of world capitalism is no different from the old in that it perpetuates extreme inequality among classes and groups within nations and among nations. Marx foresaw and described capitalism as a world system, but what we witness today goes far beyond his vision. One especially dramatic consequence of the Marxian vision is that the process of proletarianization has become an international phenomenon. Yet the modern world displays some peculiarities that deviate in some ways from the pure Marxian vision. Industries have weakened in numbers and strength in the developed regions of the world—in part by the exportation of industrial manufacturing of products to less developed parts of the world. The massive increase in service workers in the developed countries has certainly created a service proletariat in these nations, but circumstances—mainly occupational specialization and the dispersion of interests—have always conspired, in different ways, to weaken the class impulse in the service sectors.

- The victory of the forces of the new capitalism is not complete. It continues to confront competing systems that are threatened or discredited but continue to reassert themselves. Two examples will suffice. First, the national impulse struggles against the international. In some of the developed countries, nationally based capital finds itself in alliance with nationally based labor movements, both protesting against the forces of economic internationalization and pressing for limitations on the internationalization of the movements of the factors of production (including labor) and free international trade. Second, in those areas of the world, notably the former Soviet Union and Eastern Europe, the dominant voice is that of new world capitalism. Yet the apparently headlong rush to market systems evident after 1989 has met resistances from forces inherited from the communist and socialist traditions of those countries. We thus observe the apparently contradictory results of favoring wage labor, the profit system, and the consumer economy but at the same time favoring socialist-type guarantees (mainly in the form of welfare) that reduce the risks and inequalities that have always been built into market capitalism. There does not seem much doubt about which set of forces will ultimately prevail, but the contemporary scene continues to manifest ambivalence toward and a continuing political struggle among them.

- The first and third revolutions—growth through world economic capitalism and the new subnational solidarities—undermine the nation-state and nationally based political democracy in complex and subtle ways. Three of these ways, mentioned in a different context in the last chapter, should be stressed.

(1) The sovereignty of the state is being eroded by the world capitalist forces that reduce its control over its own economic and political affairs. It is extremely difficult for single states to act as a decisive influence over international economic forces that drive, in large part, their internal economic affairs: the policies and activities of multinational corporations, banks, and international agencies such as the International Monetary Fund; fluctuations in world production, trade, and capital flows; fluctuations in exchange rates. Yet the political survival of democracies and other kinds of polities depends in significant part on their capacity to affect, if not control, the economic fortunes of their citizenry. The contradiction is between the international forces that affect nations and the diminished political capacity to control those forces.

(2) The drive toward both economic growth and political democracy acts almost universally to increase economic and political expectations on the part of individual citizens and groups

in society. Both these forces translate into political pressures on governments to sustain growth, productivity, and prosperity in their own countries. Political leaders struggle to accommodate such demands in the interest of their own survival, and the spiral is completed as they strive to generate continued growth. The contradiction here is the unending and irreversible drive toward growth in the interests of satisfying relevant political constituencies—a cycle through which a point of stability and satisfaction is never reached.

(3) Subnational cultural groupings and social movements dedicated to principle, while competitors for loyalty with the nation-state, also make political demands on nation-states. I outlined the special difficulties created by these kinds of demands toward the end of the last chapter.

- A further tension arises between the forces of internationalization and the forces of localization. While internationalization proceeds apace along all fronts—production, trade, and finance; regional alliances and governments; the growth of an international community; and the diffusion of syncretic international culture—the world has also seen a resurgence of localism, as subnational groups primarily assert their own cultural identity and integrity and, in some cases, link these demands with pressures for political autonomy (including new statehood in some cases) and increased local economic self-sufficiency. Many of these movements must be regarded as economically and culturally nonrational, even irrational, because they work to isolate localities from the world economic scene and sometimes threaten to impoverish them. Yet that realization does not diminish their force and importance.

- The forces and contradictions outlined—pressures for economic growth, increased and accelerating demands on polities, and the defensive efforts of polities to contain, manage, and to some degree satisfy these demands—all point in directions that run contrary to the environmental survival of the human race in the long run. Those with optimism argue that one way out of this apparent collision course is more technology; that is to say, technology is the route to population control and increased productivity to encounter the environmental devastation. The view is not without some merit, and some examples could be provided. Be that as it may, we have not seen the necessary reversals of direction as yet, and the present course of economic and political developments point more toward environmental destruction than environmental salvation.

MECHANISMS AND PROCESSES INVOLVED IN THE INTERNATIONALIZATION PROCESS

So much for the major directions of the most important changes on the contemporary global scene. What are the main mechanisms and processes involved, and how might we best frame our understanding of them?

Specialization, Differentiation, and Interdependence

In the last chapter, I directed attention to the continuing theoretical and empirical relevance of societal structural differentiation and its multiple manifestations. The same theoretical problem surfaces internationally, though our conceptualization and concern with it has to be altered and tailored at that level.

The tradition of international economics, tracing to the mercantilists and Adam Smith, is based on the assumption of a world composed of national economies. The mercantilists argued that production and trade policies ought to be subordinated to the issue of national power, and Smith argued that all nations would become wealthier (and, indirectly, more powerful through that wealth) if they pursued the policies of comparative national advantage. In both the concept of the nation remained paramount (after all, Smith entitled his book *The*

Wealth of Nations). The accompanying assumption was that nations would specialize and trade with one another and that a world division of labor would evolve.

Given the international developments of the twentieth century, one wonders to what degree that model of international specialization retains its usefulness. Although nations maintain some control over economic policy, other economic agencies (especially multinational firms and the international agents that supply capital for development) impinge on this power. World specialization can change in relatively brief periods by the decisions of individual firms to move entire plants or suboperations, and they may do this selectively by investing or contracting out across national lines. The world has witnessed a greater differentiation among production, assembly, and corporate control. Often these operations are not organized by nation but, rather, cut across national lines and often bypass national governments. More and more, production of subcommodities is dispersed and located in sites different from assembly, and corporate control of both may be located still elsewhere. The cities of the world are developing new patterns of specialization not so much nationally as regionally. "Global cities" such as New York, London, Tokyo, and Paris are just that—cities oriented as much toward the world as they are toward their national economies (Sassen 1991). They sometimes overshadow national capitals, and are the locus of decisions made without reference to the welfare of the nations in which they are geographically situated. They develop new roles of internationally oriented commercial, financial, legal, and advertising services.

Correspondingly, the pattern of world specialization becomes more complicated. With the increasing internationalization of the economy, the economic interdependence has increased, but this interdependence has become differentiated to a greater degree from the political interdependence among nations. It is true that national economies still exist and that national governments, through their treasuries and banks, are still responsible for servicing trade deficits, international loans, and making good losses experienced through currency fluctuations. But as indicated earlier, they have lost effective control over this interdependence because they directly control neither regional economic arrangements nor production complexes nor international finance. As a result, governments control only partially economic decisions—and their effects—taking place within their boundaries. Students of differentiation and interdependence *within* societies have operated comfortably under the assumption that these phenomena develop within politically discrete societies. When we move to the international level, we must deal with a disjunction between economic differentiation and political control.

In sum, the global economic revolution of the last half of the twentieth century, which is surely accelerating and irreversible, has created more specialization and interdependence in the world and has complicated that pattern of interdependency because of the addition of new major actors in the economic world: multinational production and financial units and regional economies, in addition to nations. An enlarged but extremely imperfect and often unreliable global regulating apparatus (made up of a mix of coalitions of national governments, international financial combines, and the dynamics of international markets) has also risen. Finally, as Spencer (1897) and Durkheim ([1893] 1984) reminded us long ago, greater interdependence makes for greater potential fragility in a system, for the very reason that it is more *systemic*. When there is a sneeze in one part, the remainder is more likely to catch cold, and—in the extreme case—a breakdown in one part of the world, unless counteracted, can threaten the stability of the whole.

The Internationalization of Social Problems

Many social problems in the contemporary world already have an international character. The combination of the unequal distribution of both world income and world population growth (both working to the disadvantage of the less developed world) means that the great range of problems associated with poverty—malnutrition, infant mortality, deficiencies in education, and so on—are similarly differentially distributed. In addition, other international dimensions of social problems are already in evidence, and promise to become more salient as more of the world experiences the greater urbanization and population movements. The following are illustrations.

- We may expect the persistence and spread of social problems associated with Western market and urban development as other nations experience related lines of development. These problems include divorce and family instability, vice, crime, drugs, and abuse on the streets. Russia and Eastern Europe already show these signs, and there is no reason to believe that they will not increase as universal problems.

- The increased traffic of people through world migration and travel will internationalize health problems to a greater degree than they now are. Today no country can escape the AIDS menace for this reason, and the same will surely be true for any new infectious diseases.

- Much contemporary prostitution is becoming world prostitution, the most dramatic example of which is international sex tourism in South Asia.

- Many of those vast global cities (Sassen 1991) are leading the way in the creation of low-skill and low-paid service occupation masses, a new kind of "service proletariat" in the stratification system.

- Many social problems will be "created" by social forces external to the societies having the political jurisdiction and responsibility to deal with them. International sex tourism is an example—generated in large part by male tourists from developed countries but the responsibility of the Indian, Thai, and Philippine governments. The large-scale employment of low-skill female workers by multinationals in developing Third World countries—with the attendant problems of job insecurity, poverty, and gender conflict—is another. Future generations will witness an increase in externally generated problems. The phenomenon is an extension of what we have seen already—the pollution of Palm Springs, California, by smog from the coastal conurbation, the injury to the Black Forest from Eastern European industrial pollution, and, most dramatically, the toxification of several Western European countries in the Chernobyl incident. Extending this principle, J. Craig Jenkins and Kurt Schock (1992) have pointed out that in recent years scholars have been referring more to global structures than to domestic conditions as explanatory factors in domestic political conflict. This internationalization of social problems and the accompanying realization that they are world systemic in character will, it is hoped, provide a major impulse for legal and other forms of international intervention.

• Social problems—and the activities of those who protest against them—will become less localized and more frequently tried in the court of international public opinion, or, more precisely, the international press. The exposure of repression in Tiananmen Square, governmental impotence in Eastern Europe, and starvation in Somalia are only illustrations of the power of the media to internationalize political and social problems in an instant.

The Dynamics of International Stratification

The greater economic specialization of the world and the faster rates of growth in some developing areas make for a certain equalization of nations, in the limited sense that, being specialized, they depend more on one another for their economic survival. Put another way, they have more power over one another; the OPEC petroleum crisis of the early 1970s demonstrated that. Yet this tendency must be regarded as an interaction with other complex and long-standing systems of established inequality along economic, political-military, and prestige lines—an interaction that defies any neat characterization such as that found in some versions of Marxist and world system analysis. The broad outlines of those systems of inequality since World War II may be described briefly as follows:

- The world *economy* emerged from World War II with a clear hegemony of the United States, the one great economic power left undestroyed. This period proved short-lived. The Western and Soviet-dominated economies became frozen in a pattern of relative insulation from one another during the decades of the military cold war—with the Eastern bloc, however, never providing a decisive economic threat. Then, in area after area, American hegemony was challenged—by the American-assisted recovery of Western Europe and Japan, by other regions in Asia, by rapid but irregular strides in newly developing countries in Latin America, China, and elsewhere. The current pattern shows a relatively weakened America, but a clear pattern of domination by the North (the combined economic power of North America, Western Europe, and Japan) over the South and over the former Soviet bloc.

- The *political-military* pattern followed a related but different course. The postwar American monopoly on nuclear weapons was neutralized in short order by Soviet developments in nuclear and missile technology. For most of the cold war the world faced a situation of rough political-military parity (made so by the capacity of both the United States and the Soviet Union to destroy one another several times over). The dominant patterns of international activity were those of mutual threat and the politics of aligning powers and keeping them aligned elsewhere in the world. The economic *dis*parity of the free world and the Soviet bloc, however, continued to be enormous, and it was that very discrepancy that proved, in the end, to undo finally an already weakening political system in the Soviet bloc. That is to

say, the American acceleration of the arms race in the 1980s created a situation the American economy could not afford and the
Soviet economy could not bear. The end of the Soviet system, of
course, had an internal political dynamic as well, but the economic collapse provided the final breaking point. Since the end
of the cold war the United States and its Western allies returned
to a point of near-nuclear monopoly once again, but that brute
political-military dominance is rendered fragile by the threat of
nuclear proliferation, the economic and political costs of international peacekeeping, a diminution of collective responsibility
after the Soviet threat receded, and the continuing nonfeasibil-
ity of actually deploying the ultimate weapons.

• The international system of *prestige* is a very real phenomenon,
correlated with but distinguishable from international economic
and political stratification. Yet it is the most elusive of the three,
and this involves more than difficulties of conceptualization and
measurement. It is certainly impossible—indeed, an error to try—
to line up nations in a prestige row from top to bottom, as one
can in ranking nations by income per capita. However, it is true
that those nations that are wealthier and most closely approxi-
mate some ideal model of political democracy are most likely to
be high in prestige. But this is only part of the story. The ideological competition of the cold war period was, in fact, a context
over the *criteria* for international prestige between the Western
and Eastern blocs.

The most evident feature of the international system—and perhaps
all systems of prestige—is that it is a *ranking-plus-ambivalence* system.
It is true that developing and less developed nations are striving to
"catch up" with the West in all respects of development and, in doing so, are consciously, tacitly, or unconsciously endowing the developed countries with higher prestige. But that attitude is always tinged
with envy, resentment, and rejection—a simultaneous retraction of that

prestige, if you will. In our consideration of this more cultural system of international stratification, then, we must always begin with the phenomenon of ambivalence—not simply emulation or rejection, but both—and then move on to a deeper understanding of that phenomenon.

The Globalization of Culture

As the complexity of the world increases and intensifies, so does the communication among its various parts. Part of this is "virtual," especially the spectacular growth of television (the cultural image medium par excellence) and electronic mail systems. Another part is increased "real" communication—in trade, finance, political dialogue, migration, tourism, and international meetings.

In connection with the increasing globalization of culture, two extreme views have emerged among scholars. The one might be called homogenization, the other contextualization. The first, represented in the work of F. A. Tenbruck, holds that television spreads a common (mainly popularized American) culture throughout the world, a culture that overwhelms all others. "Generally, individual cultures are losing their autonomy as they are being drawn into the network of electronic mass media that are instrumental in creating cross-cultural audiences, movements, issues, images, and lifestyles" (Tenbruck 1990: 205). The contextualization view has been advanced by Ulf Hannerz (1990), who argues that cultural flows are complex and involve no single pattern of imperialism, and that no matter how clear the message, the transmission of culture cannot determine the spirit in which it is received and interpreted. Individual viewers "syncretize" common messages by adapting them to their own cultural wishes, attitudes, and outlooks. The truth, as in all debates about diffusion and cultural domination, must fall in the middle. All cultural forms—technology, philosophies, ideologies, social forms such as labor unions, images of heroes and villains—give evidence of both continuity and contextual alteration as they move around the world. Accordingly, models of both increasing homogenization and continuing cultural diversity must give way to synthetic models of domination-plus-syncretism.

One question has to do with whether there has been a spread of some form of the culture of "modernization" throughout the world. The roots of the debate stem in part from the work of Max Weber, who, in a dramatic formulation, argued that a special complex of values—those found in ascetic Protestantism—constituted an especially favorable cultural base for the cultivation of a capitalist mentality, entrepreneurship, rational organization of economic activities, and, by immediate extension, economic development or modernization. Sociology and, to some degree, the other social sciences have witnessed a range of interrelated controversies related to the Weber thesis: Was Protestantism indeed an efficacious cultural force, or some kind of derivative of economic development itself? Are "functional counterparts" to Protestantism to be found in other successful cases of economic development? Can "traditional" values adapt themselves into positive forces for development? Does the development of traditional societies call for the "invention" and dissemination of new cultural standards that overshadow or replace traditional ones?

Comparative research has produced no definitive answers to these queries, and the debates promise to continue. The best formulation of this issue with respect to the contemporary global scene, in my estimation, is that of S. N. Eisenstadt (1992), who argues that there is indeed a culture of "modernization" that has spread more or less universally—but irregularly—throughout most parts of the world. His point is not the earlier, somewhat discredited formulation that the "rest" of the world is striving to become like the West. At the same time, almost all nations of the world—the developed, the newly developed, the less developed—have embraced a loose congeries of values that includes a desire for material improvement (development), some species of individualism, some version of democracy, and visible elements of nationalism or cultural-regional pride. This cultural complex is not uniform in content or form but adapts itself to, shapes, and incorpo-rates indigenous cultural traditions, and thus emerges as a powerful motive force for growth. In all cases, however, the value of modern-ization is a syncretic product, tailored to the distinctive traditions of the nation or area in which it takes root.

The Development of International Community

On this topic we may perhaps be most brief, because the development of an international community has lagged noticeably behind the other aspects of world development. Indeed, a certain kind of "cultural lag" is evident. We have seen only a limited capacity of individuals to bond in a world community that transcends that of the well-established and well-endowed communities of the nation-states, fragile as these may be at this point in history. The logic of this argument is both function-alist and normative: if the world has become more systematic in all other respects, then it is essential that it become systemic as a commu-nity, if for no other reason than to provide better regulation of the sys-temic. However, dominant contemporary forces seem to press toward the development of subnational rather than supranational communi-ties. That being said, several other observations about the develop-ment of the international community can be ventured.

- All international interaction, even war, involves the operation of at least minimal normative understandings about types of be-havior that are condoned and not condoned and limits that can-not be exceeded. Much of the cold war communication between the United States and the Soviet Union consisted of the very perilous process of continually drawing lines that could not be crossed. The most dramatic examples were the Berlin airlift and the Cuban missile crisis, but others could be cited.

- An important model of the growth of international community is found in regional alliances—the European Union is the most salient instance, but the recent increases in cooperation among the United States, Canada, and Mexico is another—in which new forms of interaction and legal regulation grow crescively but irregularly toward a new level of community with at least a minimal notion of individual membership, if not citizenship. The evolution of German nationalism toward the idea of Germany *within Europe* is a remarkable example of this. The most facilitative mechanism for this kind of growth of community is, at least initially, the mutual self-interest of nations in fostering cooperative relations. At a certain point, however, the supranational community comes to assume a reality and a logic of its own. At the moment and for the foreseeable future, however, this kind of internationalization of community remains regional, not global.

• In the last analysis, the growth of international community, if it is to endure, must involve a significant redefinition of identity—with the world or humanity as a whole as its focus, not nations, classes, castes, religions, tribes, and other units. My colleague and friend, Erik Erikson, recognized this necessity in his repeated insistence on the need of humanity—for its own survival—to shed its kaleidoscopic array of "pseudo-species." By this term he referred to the tendency of human groupings to define themselves as the "true people" and to regard all other groupings as less than human in some measure. Erikson's notion of a single world humanity identifying with one another as a single species is still hopelessly utopian in the contemporary world, and probably impossible to realize ever. It is likely that any evolution of a sense of international community cannot be of the gemeinschaft variety that Erikson's vision calls to mind. Entirely new cultural beliefs and sentiments, to say nothing of institutional arrangements, may be called for. But Erikson's conception does point to the ultimate basis for all stable community life: some consciousness of kind that leads to mutual respect, civility, and nondestructiveness.

TWO METHODOLOGICAL
MESSAGES IN CLOSING

One of the themes emerging from these essays is that the nation-state is not what it used to be, at least in its ideal-typical nineteenth-century form. That happy fusion of control of wealth, power, influence, culture, and social solidarity is in the process of diffusing to units—both supranational and subnational—that crosscut the nation-state.

The implications of these developments are apparently endless. I will trace out only two—the first having to do with the foundations of the social science disciplines, the second having to do with the comparative analysis of societies (including cross-cultural and cross-national studies).

(1) As I pointed out at the beginning of the last chapter, virtually every social science has taken some version of the national society as the basic unit and the framing context for its intellectual enterprise. The question I raise is whether these analytic bases of disciplines are growing less relevant, given the complex of changes occurring in our subject matter. Insofar as the national society becomes less and less the actual *determining* basis of behavior, interaction, and institutional life, it would seem that it becomes less and less relevant to consider it the primary *analytic base* for framing and organizing our knowledge about that social life. Perhaps it is time to demote the nation-state from its throne of analytic sovereignty correspondingly, as its real base of economic, political, integrative, and cultural sovereignty is lessened.

This is not to argue that the nation-state can or should disappear as a unit of analysis, largely because it remains and will remain, if weakening, as an organizing unit for much of institutional and collective life. However, its analytic status requires questioning along many lines, among which are the following three.

- At one time, Parsons (1951) suggested that the unit of a social system (e.g., a society) should *not* be regarded as a person, but rather as a *relational* quality among persons, namely, roles. At a later time Parsons and Smelser (1956) argued that the unit of a system should be a subsystem and that a subsystem was not a person. As things turned out, neither suggestion took very deep root in the social sciences, but they still merit reflection. In particular, if the world is regarded as a system, it is an open question as to what the basic units should be, and perhaps it should be relational qualities among nations and other units that are the focus of some lines of analysis.

- Insofar as the nation remains the fundamental unit of an international system, it will have to be redefined as a less autonomous, more porous entity. The state now appears to be a unit that "sifts" and "conditions" penetrating influences over which it has limited control, rather than "reacts" to them as an independent agency. The imagery will have to be that of state units as open systems with semipermeable membranes. This alteration would also modify our idea of equilibrium and other concepts that derive from the notion of systems with discrete units. Similarly, our analysis of the causal interaction among economic, political, social, and cultural forces may have to be cast at different levels than within the confines of nation-states.

- We may also wish to recast our ideas of cultural diversity. Diversity within nations is the subject of widespread political concern at the present time. But it must be remembered that this concern arises in the context of the nation-state as reference point. It is the nation-state that is thought to "contain" a diverse population, and it is nation-states that are regarded as the units being diversified. If the nation-state recedes as a prime contender for the loyalties of citizens—for what is "diversity" if not the pressing of nonstate, nonhomogeneous claims to loyalty and identity as alternatives to nation-state loyalty?—then our whole conceptualization of diversity will have to be modified. Similarly, received cultural notions such as national identity and national culture will have to undergo revision.

(2) Internationalization, finally, challenges our accepted modes of comparative analysis. The methodological underpinning of comparative analysis is that there exists a population of units (nations or societies) that can be compared and that associations and causal processes within these units are deemed stronger or weaker according to variations in their occurrence. From the beginning the confounding effect of the possibility of the nonindependence of cases ("Galton's problem") has been an issue in comparative studies, and it has never been satisfactorily resolved (Smelser 1976). But if it is the case that the empirical independence of "units" of the world system of "nations" is being eroded through the processes of internationalization, then Galton's problem becomes progressively more serious. In the extreme, internationalization can make a mockery of the idea that independent units are being compared, because common observed effects may not result from the internal dynamics of the national system-units but from the common effect of suprasystemic processes. At that point the comparative analyst must think of abandoning the idea of nations as "cases" in a larger "population" and instead consider them as dependent, permeable units of some kind of superordinate system. In that case comparative analysis as we frequently conduct it would lose force, as would its ancillary operations of sampling, correlational analysis, the comparison of national time series, and causal inferences based on these. What would be called for, instead, would be analyses of the "case" of the world and tracing the ramifications of dynamics within this overarching system composed of partially independent units. In this connection, we might be called on to invent new methodologies and methods of comparative analysis.

REFERENCES

Aldrich, Howard E., and Peter V. Marsden. 1988. "Environments and Organization." In *Handbook of Sociology,* edited by Neil J. Smelser. Newbury Park, Calif.: Sage Publications. Pp. 361–423.

Alexander, Jeffrey, and Paul Colomy, eds. 1990. *Differentiation Theory and Social Change: Comparative and Historical Perspectives.* New York: Columbia University Press.

Alexander, Jeffrey, Bernt Giesen, Richard Münch, and Neil J. Smelser, eds. 1987. *The Micro-Macro Link.* Berkeley: University of California Press.

Allport, Floyd H. 1924. *Social Psychology.* Boston: Houghton Mifflin.

Anderson, Benedict. 1983. *Imagined Communities: Reflections on the Origin and Spread of Nationalism.* London: Verso.

Austin, J. L. [1946] 1979. "Other Minds." In *Philosophical Papers,* 3d ed., edited by J. O. Urmson and G. J. Warnock. Oxford: Oxford University Press. Pp. 76–116.

Bales, Robert Freed. 1950. *Interaction Process Analysis: A Method for the Study of Small Groups.* Cambridge, Mass.: Addison-Wesley.

Barber, Bernard. 1983. *The Logic and Limits of Trust.* New Brunswick, N.J.: Rutgers University Press.

Becker, Gary. 1976. *The Economic Approach to Human Behavior.* Chicago: University of Chicago Press.

Becker, Gary, and Kevin M. Murphy. 1988. "A Theory of Rational Addiction." *Journal of Political Economy* 96: 675–700.

Bell, Daniel. 1960. *The End of Ideology*. New York: Free Press.

Bendix, Reinhard. [1964] 1977. *Nation-Building and Citizenship*. Berkeley: University of California Press.

Blumer, Herbert. 1951. "Collective Behavior." In *New Outline of the Principles of Sociology*, edited by A. M. Lee. New York: Barnes and Noble. Pp. 166–222.

———. 1969. *Symbolic Interactionism: Perspective and Method*. Englewood Cliffs, N.J.: Prentice-Hall.

Bourdieu, Pierre. 1984. *Distinction: A Social Critique of the Judgment of Taste*. Translated by Richard Nice. Cambridge, Mass.: Harvard University Press.

Brubaker, Rogers. 1995. "National Minorities, Nationalizing States, and External National Homelands in the New Europe." *Daedalus* 124(2): 107–132.

Cable, Vincent. 1995. "The Diminished Nation-State: A Study in the Loss of Economic Power." *Daedalus* 124(2): 23–54.

Cohen, Michael, James March, and Johan Olsen. 1972. "A Garbage Can Model of Organizational Choice." *Administrative Science Quarterly* 17: 1–25.

Coleman, James S. 1990. *The Foundations of Social Theory*. Cambridge, Mass.: Belknap Press of Harvard University Press.

Collins, Randall. 1981. "On the Microfoundations of Macrosociology." *American Journal of Sociology* 86: 984–1014.

Crozier, Michel. 1964. *The Bureaucratic Phenomenon*. Chicago: University of Chicago Press.

Dahme, Heinz-Jürgen. 1990. "On the Current Rediscovery of Georg Simmel's Sociology: A European Point of View." In *Georg Simmel and Contemporary Sociology*, edited by Michael Kaern, Bernard S. Phillips, and Robert S. Cohen. Dordrecht: Kluwer Academic Publishers. Pp. 13–37.

Dahrendorf, Ralf. 1959. *Class and Class Conflict in Industrial Society*. Stanford: Stanford University Press.

Dill, David D., and Barbara Sporn, eds. 1996. *Through a Glass Darkly: Emerging Patterns of Social Demand and University Reform*. Chapel Hill: University of North Carolina Press.

Downs, Anthony. 1957. *An Economic Theory of Democracy*. New York: Harper & Row.

Durkheim, Émile. [1893] 1984. *The Division of Labor in Society*. Translated by W. D. Halls, with an introduction by Lewis Coser. New York: Free Press.

————. [1895] 1958. *The Rules of the Sociological Method.* Edited by George E. C. Catlin. Translated by Sarah A. Solovay and John H. Mueller. Glencoe, Ill.: Free Press.

Eisenstadt, S. N. 1992. "A Reappraisal of Theories of Social Change and Modernization." In *Social Change and Modernity,* edited by Hans Haferkamp and Neil J. Smelser. Berkeley: University of California Press. Pp. 412–429.

————. 1995. "Social Structure, Culture, Agency and Change." In S. N. Eisenstadt, *Power, Trust and Meaning: Essays in Sociological Theory and Analysis.* Chicago: University of Chicago Press. Pp. 1–40.

Freud, Sigmund. [1922] 1955. "Group Psychology and the Psychology of the Ego." In *The Standard Edition of the Complete Psychological Works of Sigmund Freud,* vol. 18, edited by J. Strachey et al., London: Hogarth Press. Pp. 65–143.

Friedman, Milton. 1953. "The Methodology of Positive Economics." In *Essays on Positive Economics.* Chicago: University of Chicago Press. Pp. 3–43.

Frisby, David P. 1990. "Georg Simmel's Concept of Society." In *Georg Simmel and Contemporary Sociology,* edited by Michael Kaern, Bernard S. Phillips, and Robert S. Cohen. Dordrecht: Kluwer Academic Publishers. Pp. 39–55.

Gamson, William. 1975. *The Strategy of Social Protest.* Homewood, Ill.: Dorsey.

Garfinkel, Harold. 1967. *Studies in Ethnomethodology.* Englewood Cliffs, N.J.: Prentice-Hall.

Gerschenkron, Alexander. 1962. *Economic Backwardness in Historical Perspective.* Cambridge, Mass.: Belknap Press of Harvard University Press.

Goffman, Erving. 1959. *The Presentation of Self in Everyday Life.* Garden City, N.Y.: Doubleday Anchor.

————. 1974. *Frame Analysis.* Cambridge, Mass.: Harvard University Press.

Granovetter, Mark. 1985. "Economic Action and Social Structure: The Problem of Embeddedness." *American Journal of Sociology* 91: 481–510.

Gurr, Ted Robert. 1994. "Peoples Against States: Ethnopolitical Conflict and the Changing World System." *International Studies Quarterly* 38(3): 347–378.

Habermas, Jürgen. 1975. *Legitimation Crisis.* Boston: Beacon Press.

Hannerz, Ulf. 1990. "Cosmopolitans and Locals in World Culture." *Theory, Culture and Society* 7: 237–252.

Homans, George C. 1951. *The Human Group*. New York: Harcourt, Brace and World.

———. 1974. *Social Behavior: Its Elementary Forms*. New York: Harcourt, Brace and World.

Huntington, Samuel P. 1991. *The Third Wave: Democratization in the Late Twentieth Century*. Norman: University of Oklahoma Press.

Jenkins, J. Craig, and Kurt Schock. 1992. "Global Structures and Political Processes in the Study of Domestic Political Conflict." *Annual Review of Sociology* 18: 161–185.

Kaern, Michael. 1990. "The World as Human Construction." In *Georg Simmel and Contemporary Sociology,* edited by Michael Kaern, Bernard S. Phillips, and Robert S. Cohen. Dordrecht: Kluwer Academic Publishers. Pp. 75–98.

Katz, Elihu, and Paul Lazarsfeld. 1955. *Personal Influence*. Glencoe, Ill.: Free Press.

Killian, Lewis M. 1952. "The Significance of Multiple Group Membership in Disaster." *American Journal of Sociology* 57: 309–314.

Kornhauser, William. 1959. *The Politics of Mass Society*. Glencoe, Ill.: Free Press.

Kuznets, Simon. 1972. *Quantitative Economic Research: Trends and Problems*. New York: Harcourt Brace Jovanovich.

Lawrence, P., and J. Lorsch. 1986. *Organization and Environment,* 2d ed. Boston: Harvard Business School.

Leavitt, H. J. 1951. "Some Effects of Certain Communication Patterns on Group Performance." *Journal of Abnormal and Social Psychology* 46: 38–50.

Le Bon, Gustav. [1895] 1952. *The Crowd*. London: Ernest Benn.

Lenin, V. I. [1917] 1939. *Imperialism: The Highest Stage of Capitalism*. New York: International Publishers.

Lewin, Kurt. 1948. *Resolving Social Conflicts*. New York: Harper.

Lewis, J. David, and Andrew Weigert. 1985. "Trust as a Social Reality." *Social Forces* 63(4): 967–985.

Light, Ivan, and Stavros Karageorgis. 1994. "The Ethnic Economy." In *Handbook of Economic Sociology,* edited by Neil J. Smelser and Richard Swedberg. Princeton: Princeton University Press and the Russell Sage Foundation. Pp. 647–671.

Luhmann, Niklas. 1979. *Trust and Power*. New York: Wiley.

———. 1982. *The Differentiation of Society*. New York: Columbia University Press.

MacDougall, William. 1920. *The Group Mind.* New York: G. P. Putnam's Sons.

Malinowski, Bronislaw. 1945. *The Dynamics of Culture Change: An Inquiry into Race Relations in Africa.* New Haven, Conn.: Yale University Press.

Marsh, Robert M. 1967. *Comparative Sociology.* New York: Harcourt, Brace and World.

Marx, Karl. [1867] 1949. *Capital.* London: Allen & Unwin.

Mayhew, Leon. 1990. "The Differentiation of the Solidary Public." In *Differentiation Theory and Social Change: Comparative and Historical Perspectives,* edited by Jeffrey C. Alexander and Paul Colomy. New York: Columbia University Press. Pp. 294–322.

Mills, C. Wright. 1951. *White Collar: The American Middle Classes.* New York: Oxford University Press.

Oberschall, Anthony. 1973. *Social Conflict and Social Movements.* Englewood Cliffs, N.J.: Prentice-Hall.

Olson, Mancur, Jr. 1965. *The Logic of Collective Action.* Cambridge, Mass.: Harvard University Press.

Parkinson, C. Northcote. 1957. *Parkinson's Law.* Boston: Houghton Mifflin.

Parsons, Talcott. 1951. *The Social System.* Glencoe, Ill.: Free Press.

———. 1961. "Some Considerations on the Theory of Social Change." *Rural Sociology* 16(3): 219–239.

———. 1963a. "On the Concept of Political Power." *Proceedings of the American Philosophical Society* 107: 232–263.

———. 1963b. "On the Concept of Influence." *Public Opinion Quarterly* 27(1): 37–62.

———. 1966. *Societies: Evolutionary and Comparative Perspectives.* Englewood Cliffs, N.J.: Prentice-Hall.

———. 1968. "On the Concept of Value-Commitments." *Sociological Inquiry* 38(2): 135–160.

Parsons, Talcott, and Neil J. Smelser. 1956. *Economy and Society.* London: Routledge and Kegan Paul.

Piore, Michael, and Charles Sabel. 1984. *The Second Industrial Divide.* New York: Basic Books.

Portes, Alejandro. 1994. "The Informal Economy and Its Paradoxes." In *Handbook of Economic Sociology,* edited by Neil J. Smelser and Richard Swedberg. Princeton: Princeton University Press and the Russell Sage Foundation. Pp. 426–449.

Powell, Walter W., and Paul J. DiMaggio, eds. 1991. *The New Institutionalism in Organizational Analysis.* Chicago: University of Chicago Press.

Putnam, Robert, with Robert Leonardi and Raffaella Y. Nanetti. 1993. *Making Democracy Work: Civic Traditions in Modern Italy.* Princeton: Princeton University Press.

Roethlisberger, Fritz, and W. F. Dickson. 1939. *Management and the Worker.* Cambridge, Mass.: Harvard University Press.

Ross, Edward Alsworth. 1916. *Social Psychology.* New York: Macmillan.

Sassen, Saskia. 1991. *The Global City: New York, London, Tokyo.* Princeton, N.J.: Princeton University Press.

Schlegloff, Emanuel A. 1987. "Between Macro and Micro: Contexts and Other Connections." In *The Micro-Macro Link,* edited by Jeffrey C. Alexander, Bernhard Giesen, Richard Münch, and Neil J. Smelser. Berkeley: University of California Press. Pp. 207–234.

Shils, Edward A., and Morris Janowitz. 1948. "Cohesion and Disintegration in the Wehrmacht." *Public Opinion Quarterly* 22: 280–315.

Sica, Alan. 1988. *Weber, Irrationality, and Social Order.* Berkeley: University of California Press.

Simmel, Georg. 1965. *Conflict,* translated by Kurt H. Wolff, and *The Web of Group Affiliations,* translated by Reinhard Bendix, with a foreword by Everett C. Hughes. New York: Free Press.

———. [1900] 1978. *The Philosophy of Money.* Translated by Tom Bottomore and David Frisby. London: Routledge and Kegan Paul.

———. 1984. *On Women, Sexuality, and Love.* Translated and with an introduction by Guy Oakes. New Haven: Yale University Press.

Skolnick, Jerome. 1969. *Politics of Protest.* New York: Simon & Schuster.

Smelser, Neil J. 1959. *Social Change in the Industrial Revolution.* Chicago: University of Chicago Press.

———. 1962. *Theory of Collective Behavior.* New York: Free Press.

———. 1964. "Toward a Theory of Modernization." In *Social Change: Sources, Patterns, and Consequences,* edited by Amitai Etzioni and Eva Etzioni. New York: Basic Books. Pp. 258–274.

———. 1976. *Comparative Methods in the Social Sciences.* Englewood Cliffs, N.J.: Prentice-Hall.

———. 1991. *Social Paralysis and Social Change.* Berkeley: University of California Press.

Smith, Adam. [1776] 1937. *The Wealth of Nations.* New York: Modern Library.

Smolker, R. A., A. F. Richards, R. D. Connor, and J. W. Pepper. 1992. "Sex Differences in Patterns of Association among Indian Ocean Bottlenose Dolphins." *Behaviour* 123: 38–69.

Snow, David A., and Robert D. Benford. 1992. "Master Frames and Cycles of Protest." In *Frontiers in Social Movement Theory,* edited by Alton D. Morris and Carol McClurg Mueller. New Haven: Yale University Press. Pp. 133–155.

Snow, David, E. Burke Rochford, Jr., Steven K. Worden, and Robert D. Benford. 1986. "Frame Alignment Processes, Micromobilization, and Movement Participation." *American Sociological Review* 52(4): 464–481.

Spencer, Herbert. 1897. *Principles of Sociology.* New York: D. Appleton.

Swidler, Ann. 1986. "Culture in Action: Symbols and Strategies." *American Sociological Review* 51: 273–288.

Symington, M. M. 1990. "Fission-Fusion Social Organization in Ateles and Pan." *International Journal of Primatology* 11: 47–61.

Tenbruck, F. A. 1990. "The Dream of a Secular Ecumene: The Meaning and Limits of Policies of Development." *Theory, Culture, and Society* 7: 193–206.

Tocqueville, Alexis de. [1835] 1945. *Democracy in America.* New York: Knopf and Random House.

Touraine, Alain. 1991. *Facing the Future.* Paris: UNESCO.

Treiman, Donald J. 1977. *Occupational Prestige in Comparative Perspective.* New York: Academic Press.

Turner, Ralph, and Lewis Killian. 1957. *Collective Behavior.* Englewood Cliffs, N.J.: Prentice-Hall.

Wallerstein, Immanuel. 1974. *The Modern World-System.* Vol. 1: *Capitalist Agriculture and the Origins of the European World-Economy in the Sixteenth Century.* New York: Academic Press.

Weber, Max. [1904–1905] 1958. *The Protestant Ethic and the Spirit of Capitalism.* Translated by Talcott Parsons. New York: Charles Scribner's Sons.

———. 1968. *Economy and Society: An Outline of Interpretive Sociology.* Edited by Guenther Roth and Clause Wittich. New York: Bedminster Press.

———. 1969. "'Objectivity' in Social Science Policy." In *The Methodology of the Social Sciences,* edited and translated by Edward A. Shils and Henry A. Finch, with a foreword by Edward Shils. New York: Free Press.

Williamson, Oliver. 1985. *The Economic Institutions of Capitalism: Firms, Markets, Relational Contracting.* New York: Free Press.

————. 1993. "Calculativeness, Trust, and Economic Organization." *Journal of Law and Economics* 36: 453–486.

Wolff, Kurt H., ed. 1950. *The Sociology of Georg Simmel.* Glencoe, Ill.: Free Press.

Wrangham, R. W., and B. B. Smuts. 1980. "Sex Differences in the Behavioral Ecology of Chimpanzees in Gombe National Park, Tanzania." *Journal of Reproduction and Fertility* (Supplement) 28: 13–31.

Zald, Meyer, and Roberta Asch. 1966. "Social Movement Organizations: Growth, Decay, and Change." *Social Forces* 44: 327–341.

INDEX

actors, economic model of, 16–20, 23
aesthetics, and sociology, 3–4
affirmative action programs, 62
agency theory, 14, 35
Allport, Floyd, 30
analysis: experimental vs. clinical
   modes of, 4; quantitative vs. qualitative, 4
Aristotle, 70
arts, and sociology, 3–4
Asch, Roberta, 42
ascription, 80
associations. *See* mesosociology
Austin, John, 6

Barber, Bernard, 22
Becker, Gary, 18
behavior, scientific emphasis on, 4
behaviorism, 9, 13–14
Bell, Daniel, 66
Bendix, Reinhard, 75
Berkeley, George, 6
Blumer, Herbert, 41
bonding, in groups. *See* groups
Bourdieu, Pierre, 11, 66

bureaucracy, 29, 37–38. *See also*
   mesosociology

civil society, 29, 32
cognition, 21
colonialism, 75
community: international, 94–95; society as imagined, 46, 52
comparative methodology, 98. *See also*
   historical-comparative methodology
contingency model, 40
Coser, Lewis A., x
crowd behavior, 30, 41. *See also* social
   movements
Crozier, Michel, 56
culture: globalization of, 92–94; of
   modernization, 93–94; revision of
   notion of, 53; and society, 50

democracy: international revolution in,
   78–79, 83–84; macrosociological
   problematics of, 70–72
demographic trends, and diversity, 60
dependency theory, 75–76
developing societies, dynamics of, 74

Text:	11/15 Granjon
Display:	Granjon
Index:	Barbara E. Cohen
Composition:	Prestige Typography
Printing and binding:	BookCrafters